TO LOVE, HONOR,
AND
Betray

TO LOVE, HONOR,
AND
Betray

The Secret Life of Suburban Wives

STEPHANIE GERTLER
AND ADRIENNE LOPEZ

HYPERION

NEW YORK

Library of Congress Cataloging-in-Publication Data

Gertler, Stephanie.
    To love, honor, and betray : the secret life of suburban wives / by Stephanie Gertler and Adrienne Lopez.
        p. cm.
    ISBN: 1-4013-0118-5
    1. Adultery—United States. 2. Women—United States—Social conditions. 3. Suburbs—United States. 4. Marriage—United States—Psychological aspects. I. Lopez, Adrienne. II. Title.

HQ806.G47 2005
306.73'6'0973—dc22

2004054308

Hyperion books are available for special promotions and premiums. For details contact Michael Rentas, Manager, Inventory and Premium Sales, Hyperion, 77 West 66th Street, 11th floor, New York, New York 10023, or call 212-456-0133.

FIRST EDITION

10 9 8 7 6 5 4 3 2 1

To my mother, Mary Gardner Lopez
—I MISS YOU MORE TODAY THAN YESTERDAY
And to my father, Dr. George A. Lopez—MY TRUE SURVIVOR
—AL

For the strong and courageous women I love dearly
My mother, Anna Paull Gertler
My daughter, Elyena Paull Schiffer
—SG

TO LOVE, HONOR,
AND
Betray

INTRODUCTION

⁂

To Love, Honor, and Betray was conceived one night as we sat at a local haunt in our Westchester, New York, suburb. We were sipping Cosmopolitans and talking about marriage and how few really good marriages we know—and wondering if the ones that appear to be "good" in fact are. We remarked on how many of the women we know are dissatisfied, disappointed, and disillusioned. And then we wondered how many of them are just sitting there and tolerating their marriages without any sort of diversion, for lack of a better word. Hesitantly at first, we finally acknowledged that each of us knew at least a half-dozen women who have had an affair, are having an affair, or wish they could. Imagine, we thought, if we could get these women to share with one another, to come forth, and comfort one another instead of hiding behind the public front they present to their communities.

Our conversation picked up speed: If this was happening in our insular suburban community, it must be happening across the country. We didn't want to get a sampling just from our area. We wanted to take it from coast to coast. We figured we could network through friends and come up with Mrs. A to Mrs. Z, guaranteeing our alphabetic participants not only complete anonymity but also a forum where they could come clean and explain, and as it turned out in most cases, simply to cry. We decided to focus on suburban women, primarily because it is our social orientation, and the place we two urban transplants have called home for nearly two decades. Additionally, there is an illusion about the suburbs that reeks of both isolation and utopia. Perhaps there is more scrutiny of our peers and neighbors in the suburbs, where it's more difficult to get lost and maintain our privacy within our small communities, as opposed to the sprawling cities where apartment doors shut without access to views over fences. The truth is, the white picket fences surrounding manicured lawns present a false sense of safety and perfection. The fences are far from protective. In fact, the contrary is true: They ultimately can become prisons for the women who live behind them. This goes right to the heart of the suburban stereotype. Women in the suburbs are not spoiled and not isolated. They are not dissimilar in their hearts and minds to their urban counterparts. They are not willing to become Stepford wives.

We networked through friends and family, and the response was astounding. Roughly sixty-five women were interested in participating in the book, although after vetting them, we narrowed the count down to thirty-five, and from those, we arrived at our twenty-six. Although many of the interviewees met us reluctantly at first, by the time the interview was over, there was a palpable sense of relief and catharsis in addition to a strong sense of trust. Ranging in age from thirties to seventies, they are the proverbial "all shapes and sizes." They are stay-at-home mothers, physicians, lawyers, doctors of philosophy, writers, musicians, artists, and businesswomen. They have many common denominators: They crave passion and intimacy, sex, conversation, and romance. Most have children; a few do not. Most of their marriages started out with promises they intended to keep and dreams they hoped to realize. A number of women admitted that they weren't so much in love with their husbands when they married as they were hounded by the loud ticking of their biological clocks, and they were afraid to wait any longer for the right man to come along.

Few of these women want to break up their homes, and few have. Even those in the throes of affairs are reluctant to break up their marriages, their homes, and displace their children. It is fair to say that *all* of them suffer a secret pain of one form or another. Some of that pain is a result of guilt over the affair (whether past or current) or over their desire to have an affair. In most cases, the women love their husbands despite their desires to go outside the marriage for a satisfying relationship. Their pain appears to stem from a dream they had as they walked down the aisle, and the feeling they have now that the dream has little hope of coming true. Ironically, those who merely fantasize about having affairs or lovers as they lie beside their husbands feel equally unfaithful and are perhaps more guilt-ridden than those who are having or have had affairs.

The book is divided into three categories: Women who are "Doing That," those who have "Been There, Done That," and those who "Would Like to Do That." We felt this would not only give a compelling overview of the various phases of infidelity, but it would track the commonality that we instinctively sensed: The equation that leads to infidelity is one in which fatigue, frustration, anger, and ennui add up to a reliance on fantasy—either in the flesh or in the mind—that helps get the women through the night.

This book neither advocates nor condemns adultery. It is not a book about forgiveness, redemption, or how to improve your marital love life. It doesn't make excuses or give justification for adultery. In other words, it's not judgmental. It's real stories from twenty-six married or previously married women whose marriages have not lived up to their expectations—women who wanted a marriage in which the bond transcended a binding paper document.

With the publication of Betty Friedan's *The Feminine Mystique* in 1963, a previously undefined female epidemic—termed "the problem that had no name"—was finally diagnosed. Now another of women's unnamed "problems" is out with a lusty twist. Sexual desire among married women is a fact that isn't going away and often isn't satisfied within the bonds of marriage. Women want and yearn and feel justified in doing so. Yet despite the openness of our society, where women's desires are sensationalized in glossy magazine stories, many of the women who confided in us had never confided in either their therapists or their friends. Clearly, for many women, extramarital sex is still the last taboo.

Perhaps some of what is happening in today's marriages is a sociological accident: As decades have passed since publication of *The Feminine Mystique,* the suburban marriage often has not one but two weary commuters, both of whom suffer arduous days and, often, an equally taxing commute. Additionally, suburban housewives who spend their days driving kids to school and sports, supervising play dates and waiting on supermarket lines, feel justifiably lonely (and perhaps even resentful) as their commuter husbands have cocktails after work and meetings that run late, rarely make it home on time for supper, and generally come home all but drained. The childless marriage needs nurturing as well, since there are no offspring to use as an excuse to stay together. It's been said a hundred times before that marriage takes work—a concept that runs in direct conflict with the romantic premise on which most marriages were formed, begging the question, why should it be so arduous to maintain what once felt so effortless?

The idyllic depiction of the suburban marriage, with the Nelsons, the Cleavers, and the Stones (twin beds notwithstanding), is no longer. It's taken a hit on multiple fronts: The housebound wife and mother needs and wants and feels entitled to the companionship of her husband at the end of her tiresome day, but he's too tired for conversation, let alone sex. He wants to have dinner, read the paper, and go to bed. The working mother suffers the same dismal evening as her stay-at-home counterpart, coupled with a hard day at the office and a day that starts over again with the kids when she walks in the door at six o'clock and the sitter heads for the hills. By the time dinner, baths, and homework are done, does either husband or wife have anything left? Sadly, in so many cases, no. It would be nice to think there could be solace in lovemaking at the end of a day. In other words, as much as many of these twenty-six women want sex, what they want even more is intimacy, both physical and emotional, culminating in sex where orgasm is a comprehensive statement, not merely a perfunctory release.

Emotional, cerebral, and intellectual foreplay is sorely missing from many marriages. Meanwhile, it's something that the women in this book have found with a lover who doesn't carry the same baggage as they and their husbands cart around—where the mortgage, the bills, the kids, and the in-laws don't come to bed with them. For the most part, the marriages depicted here are, in a word, lonely. Romance and hope have gone out the window. Passion is dulled by exhaustion. The once passionate couple has devolved into Mom and Dad. The stereo in the bedroom has been replaced by the baby monitor, and candles have become a fire hazard. The belle of the ball has become the old ball and chain, and the prince has become less charming. In some cases, he's turned back into a frog, and even a kiss can't seem to break the spell; in other cases, the princess no longer wants to kiss the frog because she feels that he has emotionally and intellectually abandoned her. "We don't talk anymore" is a common plaintive cry. There is a sad but rampant conclusion that not all of us grow together as we and our marriages age—some of us grow apart.

There are other reasons as well, some beyond the realm of the status quo and the expected. Although one woman has a satisfactory sex life and intellectual camaraderie with her husband, she complains that he's a mechanical and technical lover; although she tolerates him, she craves men who are more imaginative and less inhibited. Another woman took comfort in an affair as a result of her husband's insidious emotional abuse and subsequent physical abuse. Then there are those women who are deeply and hopelessly in love with other men, who now confess that they married because they wanted children. This phenomenon is particularly telling from a societal and medical point of view, since twenty-five years ago, a woman approaching her thirtieth birthday believed that her biological clock was about to cease ticking. Now, of course, women are having babies in their forties, and artificial insemination allows for conception without live-in partners or husbands. Other women feel their husbands are no longer the same men they appeared to be before financial obligations and/or children usurped romance. Many of the women we interviewed feel they, too, have changed over the course of their marriages. There are women who seek comfort in either fantasies or real-life lovers. They wait for the right moment to leave, and yet as deeply in love as they are with others, they stay because the pull of the familiar, the unraveling of finances, the children are all factors that keep them living cloak-and-dagger lives in which weekends away from their lovers are fraught with emptiness and longing.

One question remained as the women cried and searched their souls and feared the uncertainty of their futures, both with their lovers and their husbands. Why are these bright, dynamic, loving women still in marriages that leave them feeling empty and longing for more? Why and when did dreams and romance and desire vanish? Above all, why can't they leave or, the flip side, why do they stay? The answers were simple and straightforward: either because of the children, or because the devil they know is better than the devil they don't. For some, the reason to stay is financial: They have become materially comfortable, and they fear that their lifestyles will be compromised if they leave. Many stay because they're still holding on to the hope that things could get better.

One of the most compelling (and revealing) moments was when the following question was posed to women who are currently having affairs: "If you walked in the door tonight and the hallway was lit with votive candles leading you on a romantic path to the kitchen where a pot of stew simmered on the stove . . . and the table was set with candles and a bottle of wine . . . and there was your husband, waiting for you . . . and he said, 'You need to tell me what you want and I'll listen. You need to teach me how to make love to you—I love you and I don't want to lose you' . . . What would you do? Would you stay with your lover?" After the question was posed, each woman cried and, without hesitation, said she would want to stay with her husband and make it work. In other words, the vast majority of the interviewees still want the fairy tale.

This is nothing new. We can trace marital infidelity back through the centuries, through fiction and nonfiction—Bathsheba, Madame Bovary, Hester Prynne, Ingrid Bergman, Guinevere, Francesca Johnson. The women we present are neither celebrities nor fictional protagonists; they are all quite real and no different from the rest of us.

In no way do we pretend to have achieved expert status on the subject of adultery. We are reporters with neither sociological nor psychological expertise. We are not citing statistics or data. Our only credentials are that we are women who are or have been married. Each of these women struck a nerve within us. We cried with some of them, some astonished us, some made us angry on their behalf. We wished we could help them extricate themselves from marriages that are clearly, from the outsider's point of view, long over.

We hope this intimate book will bring comfort to women who find themselves in similar situations to our twenty-six participants, who are neither saints nor sinners. We hope it will affirm to both men and women that marriage should be, and can be, more than a writ, a notarized piece of paper that binds us.

We wonder if husbands who read this book will suspect whether their wife is, or could be, one of the twenty-six. We wonder if it will give them pause—or if they'll put the newspapers in front of their faces and assume that their wives couldn't possibly have a secret life.

Doing That

Taking Chances

There is a great deal of rationalization, and a laundry list of justifications, running through this group of women. There is also confusion, which appears to stem from a guilt that they strive to suppress on what might be a minute-to-minute basis—with the exception of one woman, who compares her infidelity to a man's and says she hasn't the slightest twinge after she sleeps with another man and then crawls into bed beside her husband later that night. However, it appeared to be either their denial of guilt, or their resistance to guilt, that has propelled them through their affairs. They seek a fantasy that departs from what is too often a painful and seemingly insoluble reality.

What so many don't seem to address are the repercussions, should the affair be revealed. They choose not to ponder what might happen should their affairs come to an end, and they are forced to face the fact that their marriage is still as lonely and unfulfilling. Is the affair somewhat like putting a Band-Aid on an injury that requires surgery?

The affairs, although clearly feeding the women's unrequited desires, their need for conversation, passion, and intimacy, are not providing solutions, and they are putting the women at risk of complications—

namely, destroying their own lives, the lives of their children, extended families, and even friendships. It was astounding to learn that many of the women lived in such fear of discovery that they had confided in neither a close friend nor even their therapist.

The natural question is why not tell your husband how you feel? Why not tell him that you long for conversation, for greater intimacy, for more time with him? But the question is overly simplistic. It is a vicious cycle: If the women had the sort of relationship with their husbands where issues could be aired, and cards put plainly on the table, the marriages would be, if not good, at least ones that were open enough for the husband and wife either to work together to sustain the marriage or end it amicably with the realization that it is simply not meant to be. These women felt that they not only tried to get through to their husbands but were still trying, despite their current affairs.

When their husbands responded to their grievances, the wives felt the response was perfunctory and dismissive. They were left feeling undesirable, hurt, and emotionally unsafe. The irony is that nothing is more unsafe than an affair, a state of being they don't always realize when they embark on the affair, but come to realize as it picks up speed. There is also a sense that the precarious nature of the affair is an aphrodisiac of sorts. Meeting the lover at a hotel, whether for a night or a weekend, is tantamount to taking an illegal drug that gives you an incredible high.

The bottom line is, being married and lonely is isolating and sad. That wasn't part of the deal. Women and men marry to alleviate loneliness. When a woman finds herself in what is meant to be a permanent union with a man who, for whatever reason, leaves her cold, a kind of desperation can occur. It is a panic that she feels may be assuaged by feeding her desires, both sexually and emotionally. Once the sustenance of the affair begins, however, is she truly able to distinguish between lust and reality?

For certain, there is no physical stereotype for the woman who is having an affair. She is not dressed provocatively, wearing tight clothes and a lot of makeup, and she's not necessarily stunning in a movie-star sort of way. She looks like "the rest of us." She looks like a mother, a wife, a friend, and speaks like a woman whose heart is breaking in two.

MRS. A

Mrs. A is a fifty-one-year-old woman with two daughters aged twenty and twenty-three. An advertising agent, she lives just outside Seattle and has been married for twenty-five years. Even though the girls are out of the house—one in college and the other in nursing school—she doesn't want to leave her husband and break up their home. She looks forward to the day when she and her husband will walk their daughters down the aisle and have grandchildren coming to visit. She once thought that when the girls were more independent, she and her husband, Charlie, would travel together and have quiet, romantic evenings alone at home. But as the girls took off, so did Charlie. His hours are longer. He isn't there—not in body, mind, or spirit. The sexual and emotional intimacy she has with her lover is what she would really like to have with her husband.

It all started last summer. The third-floor bathroom leaked for years until we concluded that we couldn't put off construction. It had to be renovated and updated. I shopped around for a contractor, asking neighbors, the electrician, and the plumber, and came up with several names, none of whom called back except for one. His name was Ronnie. He promised to show up the following week, and of course, he didn't. I called him back and left my number again, and he called back after another week and left a message on the tape, and finally, we connected. He was pleasant enough on the phone but very laid-back and made no excuse for why he hadn't shown other than that he was busy with a "really big job." "Whatever," I said, sounding like a fifteen-year-old, but I was aggravated and didn't have time to hear how hard *he* was working. Another one, I thought, since all my husband did was complain about business and clients. The next day Ronnie showed up. To tell you the truth, I didn't think much of him at first. He was young—thirty-eight to my then fifty. For some reason, I had pictured him as silver-haired and older. He was wearing painter's pants and a sleeveless T-shirt, and although he was muscular and taut, he didn't impress me too much. I had a pile of work to go through that day, so I showed Ronnie the bathroom, showed him the leak in the ceiling downstairs, and left him on his own. I was quite stressed, since my summer intern had bailed out. I work for an ad agency, and angry clients were harassing me and haranguing me over work that the intern had left undone.

That day he started, in July, it was hot hot hot. I was in my office all morning and then realized it would be nice if I paid some attention to him— to ask him if he'd like a cold drink or a sandwich or something. He looked grateful when I brought him a small bowl of fruit and a bottle of Evian. He said that most people never offered him anything. For a moment, I thought he looked at me longer than he needed to, but then I thought I was being ridiculous. How could I think that this guy, who was a dozen years younger than I, was being even remotely seductive.

The truth is, at the time he worked here, my ego was in the dumps. My husband, who worked incredibly long hours, was rarely home. He's a medical malpractice lawyer. If I pinpointed when he increased his hours and workload, it was when the girls went off to college. Strange coincidence. Naturally, I felt that he simply didn't want to be one-on-one with me. The only physical contact I had with my husband was when he came home at night and crept into the bed: There was a body next to me, but it had been over a year since we had sex. I would say things to him sometimes, but he said it was all just "bad timing." He'd get angry and defensive. My female ego was wounded. One night when we were getting ready to go out, I purposefully stood in front of him in thong underwear and a lacy bra, and even that didn't get me anywhere. He made me feel so unattractive. Part of me wondered whether he was impotent, and part of me wondered whether he was gay, and another part of me wondered if he was having an affair. I figured if he was having an affair, he'd be smart enough to still have sex with me, at least as some sort of ruse. If he was gay, I thought I'd sense it . . . women can usually sense that sort of thing. And if he was impotent, well, he wasn't telling, and at that point I was afraid to test the waters, so to speak. Whatever it was, I was no longer the object of his passions. He made me feel old and foolish for even wanting sex. It was so depressing to lie in bed and listen to him snore or have him hardly acknowledge me and put down his magazine and then shut out the light. I'd go downstairs and sleep on the couch just because it pained me to sleep beside this man who had once been such a passion of mine (and I of his) and now nothing.

We had our first child just a couple of years after we married, but honestly, the passion died long before that. Truly, I think passion died on our wedding night, when I became Mrs. A. When we were living together, our sex life was great. It was like once we got married, he treated me as The Wife. I knew then that he had a lot of issues, but I figured we could work them through together. Unfortunately, if I brought up issues between us—like lack of sex and conversation and intimacy in general—he went nuts. So I kept quiet, gave him his dinner, and often cried myself to sleep.

Ronnie was in the house just about every day for a month. Much to my dismay, I started to look forward to seeing him. As the days went by, Ronnie and I chatted from time to time. He'd tell me about his wife (she was ten years older than he) and about his three-year-old daughter. He never complained about his wife, and he loved his little girl. Funny, that was when I started to find him attractive. The muscles didn't do it for me as much as what appeared to be a caring and a sensitivity when he spoke—and speaking while he was hammering and leaning over a sawhorse didn't hurt. The combination was riveting.

One day I was heading out to the store, and I asked him if he wanted anything. Coffee? Soda? Nothing, he said, and he looked up at me. "Do you ever get bored?" he asked. "Are you happy?" I felt uncomfortable. I took a deep breath and said that yes, I was bored sometimes, and no, I wasn't entirely happy. I asked him why he had asked, and he said because sometimes he would be pulling out tiles and lifting out concrete and wondering what the hell he was doing with his life. He said that when he was a kid, he had wanted to be a doctor, but he dropped out of college midway because he didn't have the money for the tuition, and he started doing construction. The money in construction was so good that he kept putting off college until he turned around at age thirty and realized this was his life and he'd blown it. That was when he met his wife—five years later, she got pregnant and they got married and now he was thirty-eight and just felt like he was going nowhere. He said he was getting too old for this kind of work. That his shoulders and his back ached at night and he was tired of being referred to as "the guy." Is "the guy" going to show up today? Is "the guy" almost finished? Ronnie made me think, and for the first time in what seemed like forever, a quiver went through me that I allowed myself to feel.

I still couldn't imagine that Ronnie found me in the least bit attractive. I figured he was talking to me like a mother figure. That was how my husband viewed me, for sure. This is crazy, I thought. He's thirty-eight and I'm fifty. There's a stigma to fifty. Even more, I figured his wife was probably a knockout, since he was so great-looking. I pictured this well-put-together sex kitten—he was so youthful and muscular that I couldn't imagine him being with an older woman unless she was drop-dead gorgeous. As it turned out, his wife wasn't gorgeous. She picked him up a few days later when his truck was giving him problems. She was *far* from gorgeous. But she was awfully sweet and nice, and it was just another aspect of Ronnie that I liked—somehow she indicated an even greater depth to him. He finished the bathroom, and a month later, Ronnie was out of my life.

Until the toilet overflowed.

I called the plumber, who blamed the whole thing on Ronnie's tile work, so I called Ronnie, who said the plumber hadn't centered the drain. The two of them showed up at the same time on a Thursday morning and had it out in the bathroom while I stood there. Finally, Ronnie said, "Look, I'm not going to argue with you anymore. I'll reset the toilet, and I'll repair the tile, because the bottom line is that Trish here is the one who's paying the price. So if you won't fix it, I will."

The plumber left, and Ronnie was my knight in shining armor. He had another job that day and couldn't come back until three. I was going out that night with my girlfriends for our once-a-month gathering at a local restaurant. It was six-thirty, and Ronnie was still there when I went to get dressed for the evening. Unlike other days, when I wore sweatpants and a torn-up tank top, I was dressed decently. Tight jeans. Nice tank top. Hair blown out. A little makeup. I went in to say that I was leaving and to lock up and I'd see him in the morning. He said I looked nice and asked where I was headed, and I told him that I was going over to the Barn on Route 17. He knew the place. He said he'd been there a couple of times because it was close to Lowe's, where he bought his supplies. I was being flip when I asked, "Why don't you stop by and have a beer?" He said he just might, as though it were a threat, and I figured he was either being polite or kidding. I honestly, I didn't take him seriously. Tight jeans or not, I was still feeling every bit fifty and undesirable. Just as he and I were having this exchange, my cell phone rang. It was Charlie, my husband, to say that he wouldn't be home until at least eleven. He said that he had a dinner meeting with clients, but who knew? And who cared? Ronnie asked if Charlie always got home late, and I said that he did. And then Ronnie said that if I were his wife, he wouldn't work so late at night. I felt myself blush. That quiver was coming back over me again. I think I nearly danced into my car, and then I felt so foolish. How could anyone find me attractive?

I met the girls and we had dinner, and as always, our group dwindled down by nine-thirty and then it was just my friend Hannah and me. I kept checking the door. I felt like such an idiot, thinking that he might show. And then, as Hannah and I told the bartender that we'd take a check, there was Ronnie.

Of course, I pretended to be totally surprised—and I was. I introduced him to Hannah and explained that Ronnie had been working in my house for the last month or so. He looked wonderful. His hair was shampooed and curled over the back of his collared shirt, and he wore dark jeans and sneakers. He sat next to me and ordered a beer and seemed very comfortable. And then Hannah started asking him a million questions, some about work and some about himself. After two beers, Ronnie went to the bathroom, and Hannah, who is usually ready to leave by ten-thirty at the latest, was going strong. Of course, she wanted to know "What gives?" She said he was really cute, and I acted innocent, like I would never give that guy the time of day. Then Hannah whispered in a stage voice, "He wants you." I told her she was crazy. But she asked if I noticed how he was looking at me. I told her that he had fixed the bathroom and that was it. I decided to ignore her.

Ronnie came back from the bathroom, and Hannah asked where he lived. His answer made her eyebrows shoot up. His home was a good thirty minutes from the Barn. She pressed him and asked if he always went to bars thirty minutes from his house. Honestly, she was like the district attorney! But Ronnie was smooth and not at all defensive. He said he had to go to Lowe's, and that was nearby. Then Hannah commented that he was pretty clean for someone who came from work, given the kind of work he does, and he said that was because his gym was nearby as well and he had worked out and then cleaned up. Hannah was like Dick Tracy, and Ronnie fielded her questions like a true gentleman, with no innuendo or indication that he was there for any other reason than coincidence.

Hannah backed down, and Ronnie bought another round. I started drinking lots of water and eating bar nuts to counteract the alcohol. I looked at my watch. It was nearly eleven. For once, my husband would be home before me. Anyway, Ronnie started talking about his thwarted dreams about medical school, and he showed a picture of his daughter, and he was just all-around entertaining and engaging. It was not planned, but at the same time, we both had to use the bathroom. We walked to the back of the restaurant, and both bathrooms were occupied. Weird, since the restaurant was nearly empty. Anyway, that was when he kissed me. He said he'd wanted to do that all night. I hadn't been kissed like that in years, let alone kissed. By the time I got out of the bathroom, he was back at the bar talking to Hannah. And then Hannah said she had to go. "Call me tomorrow," she said to me with a twinkle in her eye. About ten minutes later, Ronnie paid his check (Hannah had already paid ours), and we left.

Ronnie walked me to my car, and as I was about to open my car door, he kissed me again, leaning against me this time as I leaned against the car. He said that he wanted to see me. I said I was married, and he said, "So am I." He said he'd see me in the morning. I can't remember ever being so nervous. On the one hand, I was worried about what my husband would say once I got home. I just didn't know where any of this was heading.

The next morning I offered Ronnie coffee, and we sat in the kitchen and talked for a bit, and then he looked at me and said, "So?" I felt like a schoolgirl. I asked him if he did this sort of thing with all the women he knew around town. He could have joked or teased me, but he said no in a serious tone. He was awfully sincere, but I figured he was the world's best bullshit artist. He took my hand and walked me over to a spot in the kitchen that was away from the window, and he kissed me and ran his hands all over my body, and I just melted. We walked up the stairs to my bedroom, and although I felt a twinge that I was about to have sex with another man in the "marital bed," I remember thinking that the marital bed hadn't been marital in so long that it didn't really matter. He took off his boots and his shirt, and I saw a tattoo on his back and another on the lower part of his stomach. His muscles were rippling. His stomach was so tight. Then he took off my shirt and laid me back on the bed and stood up beside me and took off his sweatpants, and it occurred to me that I hadn't had sex in so long that I wondered if I would even remember what to do. When he made love to me, it was amazing. He was an incredible lover, and the best part was that he kept kissing me. My husband had never kissed me like that when he made love to me. I thought of the movie *Pretty Woman,* when Julia Roberts said that she wouldn't kiss Richard Gere because kissing was too intimate. I thought, Yes, kissing *is* the most intimate.

I asked Hannah to meet me that night, and when I came into the restaurant, she said I looked great. She said I looked ten years younger. She kept staring at me: "You slept with him, didn't you?" I just smiled. She said, "It's incredible what sex can do for the skin. It beats a face-lift, I swear."

The strange thing about this affair with Ronnie is that I am not in love with him, nor is he in love with me. I've never had sex with a man I didn't feel I was in love with—a man with whom I didn't have a "real" relationship that was "going somewhere." Even in college, when everyone was fairly promiscuous and free, I always had to be *in love*. There were only two boys when I was in college, one in high school, and then, after college, just two other men before I married my husband. Having an affair was not on my horizon. It wasn't guilt that stopped me, or a heightened sense of morality, it was simply that in order for me to have sex with someone, I always had to be in love with him.

Sometimes I fantasize about Ronnie and wonder what it would be like to be with him on a more permanent basis. I wonder if he would make love to me the way he does now if we, say, lived together. I have a bit of a hang-up about the age difference, though. He doesn't know how old I am, and I'm afraid to tell him. I once told him the year I was born because he asked, and I lied and now can't remember what year I told him! I don't know why I feel this way, but I think it stems from the fact that when I turned fifty, my marriage was so stale and loveless, and I felt so old and washed up. My husband makes me feel old because he doesn't want me. Sometimes I get the urge to tell him about Ronnie just to wake him up—to let him know that someone desires me and I can make love to someone with a passion. The thing is, I would prefer to have this with my husband, although there is such self-consciousness between us. Having sex with my husband now would be worse than having sex with a stranger.

Ronnie and I really don't talk very much. He comes over a day or two a week, and we have sex. Great sex. He usually gets here at noon, during his lunch hour, or before he begins the day. Sometimes I feel bad when he leaves, because it's not the kind of relationship I really want. I would prefer to have an affair that was of the heart as well as the mind. I can't tell whether or not he really likes me or whether it's all just sexual, and that's a little tough for me to reconcile. He fills a need in me, but there are others that are still longing to be filled. I would like to have it all. I'd like to be with my husband, a husband, in the same way that I am when I'm with Ronnie and we get lost in each other. Instead, my husband comes home at night and tosses his brief-case on the table and sits down to dinner and reads the newspaper or *Sports Illustrated* and complains about work. Then he puts on pajamas and gets into bed and says good night, and that's that. I doubt we will ever recapture what we had when we were dating and living together before we were married. I think it's a lost cause. I don't know exactly what I'm going to do, and I try not to think about the future, because it's too painful. I just look forward to the next time Ronnie comes by and makes me feel, for an hour or so, that I am desirable and desirous and passionate and alive. That was once my dream for me and Charlie.

MRS. B

Mrs. B is a fifty-year-old interior decorator from Buckhead, an affluent suburb of Atlanta. She has been married for eighteen years, has two teenage daughters, and her husband is an architect. She is a self-described cheater who recently got caught. She and her husband have led an opulent lifestyle, and their marriage has been strained for most of their years together. Now in the process of an acrimonious divorce, Mrs. B doesn't regret this most recent affair. She is in love with her boyfriend, and although she doesn't know whether she wants to marry or live with him, she does know she couldn't have stayed in her marriage. She says the affairs were a question of emotional and spiritual survival. With this most recent affair, in which she fell in love, she chose herself above all else—even her children.

I had my first affair six months after I was married. It lasted about two months. You see, I got pregnant two months after I was married, and my husband reacted very badly. I wanted the *I Love Lucy* episode when Ricky was so thrilled to hear that Lucy was carrying his child, or the lines from that Paul Anka song about the woman who was having his baby and how it was an affirmation of how much she loved him. Well, it was a total shock to me when my husband reacted with "How could you do this to me? What the hell have you done? You tricked me!" I fell apart. I was thirty-one and my husband was thirty-three, so it wasn't like we were children. We had a huge blowup, and one night this good friend and neighbor of mine came over to bum a cigarette, and the next thing I knew, we were having an affair that lasted five months into my pregnancy. He was the one who backed away. He questioned what he was doing, having an affair with not only a married woman but one who was having a baby. I thought I was in love with him, but looking back, I have no idea if I was. I think I just needed someone so badly at that time in my life. And I wasn't in love with my husband. I highly doubt any woman has an affair if she's dead in love with her husband. The truth is, I wasn't in love with him when we got married. On my wedding day, I turned to my sister and said, "Boy, did I just make a mistake."

Looking back, it's all so transparent. I'd invested time in my relationship with my husband—four years. Once I turned thirty, I heard the clock ticking and started to get nervous about having babies. The bottom line was, I wanted babies. I also have a streak in me that says I have to win, and marriage was the prize. Ironically, we cheated on each other the entire time we dated. I continued two affairs that started before I was married and went four years into my marriage—both men lived overseas, so I would sleep with them maybe two or three times a year, when they were stateside.

Anyway, I had the baby, and we moved to the suburbs. There was a period of about ten years when I was faithful, and during that time we had another child. My husband was a great father. I seem to recall that our relationship improved as well, and most important, we loved our babies. Moving to the suburbs presented the perfect picture. Then time goes by and you start projects, and he starts projects, and you have kids and careers and you build a house and tend the garden, and one day you look up when you think that everything is all complete, and you realize you don't know who he is, and he doesn't know who you are. I don't think I know anyone who's happily married.

My ten-year hiatus without having an affair ended. I started having serious flirtations with clients. I guess before that, I felt that I was just so gross—
the kids were young, and I didn't have time for makeup and all that. I mean,
who would have even wanted to have an affair with me? I was exhausted,
getting up at five and going to work and coming home and being Mommy. It
wasn't until I was about forty-two that I started to take care of myself again,
and I noticed that men liked me again. I even flew to Paris to be with one of
my clients. My husband and I were having sex with each other, but that was
the point when I started to dislike him so intensely that I had a difficult time
sleeping with him. I would think, Oh God, let me pretend I'm asleep. It got
to the point where I couldn't stand the way he ate, the way he breathed. We
rarely spoke. He worked weekends, and I felt more like his maid than his
wife. You go through a few years like that, and a pretty good hate comes
through. He was also constantly belittling me. I was much higher on the cor-
porate ladder than he ever was, and I still am, but he never acknowledged that.
He hated me. He felt that I wanted him to succeed professionally only for a
positive reflection on me. Sometimes I wonder if he was right, although I
thought I encouraged him for his sake.

We never should have married to begin with. The old adage that opposites
attract is bullshit, as far as I'm concerned. I think people should marry people
who are like them, not antithetical to them. He's a very serious man. He has
an odd sense of humor, and I always felt that I had to explain it to people,
telling them that what he'd said was meant as a joke. I have a huge ego. I'm
funny, strong-willed, incredibly opinionated. I was the one who would walk
into a room and take it over, and he was the one in the shadows. I like to
spend money, and he doesn't like to spend a dime. He's retiring, and I'm flam-
boyant. I'm a people person, and he's a misanthrope.

My current affair has broken up my marriage, but it was also my first
affair in which I truly fell in love. I met Jack through work about eight years
ago, and we became good friends. We'd have dinners and lunches together,

and one thing led to another. One night about a year and a half ago, we were at a business function, just as friends, and as he drove me home that night, I started kissing him, and here we are. His marriage dissolved because it was way down the tubes anyway. Divorce has been an easier road for him, however, because he has no children. I suppose that our affair was the catalyst for the dissolution of his marriage, but he knew I wasn't convinced that I wanted to dissolve *my* marriage. He didn't leave his wife for me.

I never intended this affair to break up my marriage. I was frightened by the notion that I was falling in love—maybe for the first time in my life. And I am still so in love with this man, it's like I can't even see. While in the throes of my affair, I told my husband that we needed to address the fact that our marriage wasn't working, and I suggested that we separate and give it a break. I confessed that I questioned whether or not I loved him anymore. I had no intention of confessing and telling him that I was having an affair. That is rule number one. Never, never confess. Well, the next thing I knew, he refused to move out of the house. Even at that point, even though I felt there was no love between us, even though I was in love with another man, I still wasn't certain that I wanted to end my marriage. I was so conflicted. I felt separation would be the one thing that would tell me what I wanted and where my husband and I stood with each other. I felt I had no partner in marriage and no partner in parenting. But I wasn't sure I was willing to pay the price that would break up my home.

One night I came home from work around nine o'clock. I'd been at a business party with Jack. My daughters greeted me at the door crying and screaming. They said that Dad had told them I was having an affair, and that I would want custody of them only if I could get child support. They were hysterical, and I was hysterical. I talked to them, and I said it was true that I was having an affair. How could I have denied it? Obviously, I'd been caught. Somehow I'd been found out, and if I had denied it that night, they would have found out a week or a month later, and my deceit would have been even greater. I told them I had fallen in love with someone, but that I wanted them and not just because I would get money. They reacted terribly. They were brokenhearted. My oldest asked how I could do that to her father, and I answered that she was old enough to see that I had fallen out of love with her father, and he with me. Now she understands, and although it's been a painful road, she supports my decision.

I confronted my husband that night. He'd hired a private investigator who had followed Jack and me to hotels and restaurants, and there were pictures of us together. He knew Jack's name, his wife's name, his address. He knew nearly everything. It was all documented. My husband was not only filing papers that would be served on me the next day, he was also filing papers on Jack.

Now, understand that the only person I had confided in was my very best friend of nearly twenty years to whom I've always told all my secrets. I later found out that she was the one who had betrayed me. When I called to tell her that my husband had found out, she acted strangely, but I still couldn't believe that she was the one, even though I knew it couldn't have been anyone else. She acted too surprised, but her surprise was disingenuous. And then someone else in town came up to me, someone I knew superficially, and said, "If you think this woman has been your best friend for the last twenty years, you're wrong. Don't trust her." Well, then I knew. And in the last six months, she's become my husband's "best friend." It took me so long to connect the dots. I'm going to tell you something—and it's going to sound funny coming from a woman who cheats—but I'm a really loyal person. I'm a really loyal friend. I would always defend my friends. I won't let anyone dis them in front of me and talk behind their backs. Everyone has quirks and flaws. What my so-called best friend did, in spite of my infidelity, was destroy my marriage. Despite the affair, despite the fact that I was in love with another man, who knows? I still may have stayed in my marriage.

I'm still at the house every weekend with my girls, and my husband gets home (as he always did) around ten o'clock. I keep an apartment in Atlanta and stay there during the workweek. My husband told me that if I didn't get out, he'd make it a nasty custody battle. On the weekends when my husband is working, I stay over at the house, but I sleep in the nanny's room.

It's like the *War of the Roses*. We're still not divorced, and the process is brutal. But I want to be with my kids. The relationship I have with my girls now is beautiful. I won't introduce them to Jack yet, though. They know of him, and know that we're together, but it's not the right time yet to bring him into their lives.

I have to confess, after everything hit the fan, I needed the break from the house and the kids. I needed the space to see where the hell I was in my life. I didn't want to be the cliché: the divorced woman who stayed at home with her kids in the suburbs and never had a date. I guess that's selfish, but I'm selfish. Besides, I couldn't have been that martyred, sainted woman, because I am not that woman in so many other aspects of my life. I felt that I would die if I was working all day and then running home to the suburbs all by myself and never seeing anyone or doing anything again. So, despite my husband's threats, I was happy to have the apartment in the city. I have to be honest. In the last three years, affair or no affair, I got home so late at night during the week, I had drifted away from that lifestyle. And by the time I got home at night, the kids were either asleep or on the computer, and it didn't matter whether I was home or not.

I'm a veritable pariah in Buckhead now. The fallen woman who had an affair and left behind her poor, sweet, adorable husband and children. I don't have a best friend in Buckhead anymore. I hate her so much. But I wonder, what does all this say about me? Am I just the worst judge of character? Believe it or not, I feel that my best friend's betrayal of me is worse than my betrayal of my husband.

It's all very complicated, and there is that huge regret—I wish I had been a better wife, and I wish he had been a better husband. But I can't regret where I am right now, because for the last ten years, certainly the last five years, I have been so lost. I had lost any kind of real feeling, and when you fall in love, it magnifies that feeling of being lost.

I believe that most women who have affairs at least *think* they're in love at the time. I think women generally fall in love easier than men do. For me, I never felt any guilt about any of the affairs I've had. I often said that I'm like a man—I can fuck men the way men fuck women, without any guilt—and get right back into bed with my husband at night without the slightest tinge of remorse.

The other affairs I had gave me something else. You see, the minute you get married and have a child, you become Mother. Those other men never knew me as Mother. To them, I was a sexual being again, something that was lost after I had kids. With this man, it's even more different. I love him, and I had forgotten how great sex could really be.

But you know what? As satisfied and gratified as I am, as happy as I am, I'm still not convinced that I wouldn't cheat on Jack somewhere down the road. I think after you've cheated the first time, you come to know the type of person that you are. When you realize how easy it is to cheat, and how it feeds your ego, it just becomes easier for the rest of your life to be a cheater. Men know this, and people accept this about men. And the chance you take when you're cheating is an aphrodisiac. For me, cheating is also conquest. It's the ultimate win. The *ultimate* conquest. But I have one major question: Why is it that when a man cheats on his wife, the community and friends and family expect the wife to suck it up and take it? Why isn't the same true for women? Is it because men can't be one-upped by a woman? I mean, why are men forgiven, and women ostracized and isolated?

Mrs. C

*Mrs. C is forty-nine years old. She lives in a suburb of Manhattan
with her husband and their twin daughters, who are now fifteen. A
dentist with a fairly busy local practice, she is vibrant and emotional
and intelligent. She speaks eloquently, articulately, and self-
analytically, yet also from the bottom of her heart. Her eyes well up
with tears when she speaks about her marriage, and they sparkle when
she speaks about her lover, her second during the course of her twenty-
two-year marriage. Her affairs, especially the current one, were never
as much about sex as they were about conversation, attention, and
being with someone who heard her when she spoke. Despite the hope
she has for the future with the man she loves, she is also afraid: Once
she thought her future was carved in stone, and although she and her
lover vow to be together and leave their marriages, there is still an air
of uncertainty. She says that she cannot stay in her marriage much
longer, but she worries about the financial repercussions of divorce
and the effect that it might have on her children. Cloak-and-dagger
meetings with her lover, which take place every three weeks or so, give
her something to look forward to; and then, like Cinderella, she goes
back home.*

I married Tom when I was in dental school. We met at a bar in New York City. He was at business school in Boston at the time and was visiting friends for an extended spring break. It turned out that we had both gone to University of Massachusetts, and we both had taken the same course about James Joyce. It was a small class, yet I never remembered seeing him there. We talked that night at the bar, and he asked me out, and we spent the next week seeing each other every day and just talking for hours and hours. We came to realize that we had a lot of friends in common from UMass, and our family backgrounds were similar. We were both from the New York area. By the end of the week, I knew I could fall in love with him. He went back to Boston, and I didn't hear from him for quite a while. I knew he had a girl-friend there, but I was still pretty heartbroken. Then, a couple of months later, he broke up with the girlfriend. He had finished his degree. It was May, and he'd landed a job in New York at a brokerage house. We saw each other, of course, and we fell in love.

At the time I met Tom, I knew this other guy—Brian. Brian and I went all the way back to our days at UMass. He was in graduate school there and one of the first people I ever met who lived like a real person. He had a real job and a house and a dog, and we used to go barreling around in his VW bus. He was bright and funny, and I enjoyed his company, but we were never in the same place at the same time, either spiritually or geographically. He ended up taking a Ph.D. at the University of Wisconsin, and I missed him. I couldn't help but think that he was a man I could see spending a much longer period of time with. A few months after Brian moved, and just a cou-ple of weeks before I met Tom, I wrote a letter to Brian asking him if I should take my boards in Wisconsin when the time came. I was sending out more than obvious hints that I wanted a serious relationship with him— more than just sleeping together. I wanted more definition in our relation-ship. Well, Brian never answered my letter. What I didn't know at the time and discovered later was that he had met a woman at UMass and she had moved out there to be with him. I think he viewed our relationship as a friendship—you know, friends who sometimes slept together. He had been burning the candle at both ends, apparently: having this other relationship going on and me at the same time. Of course, he didn't owe me that information, since we were just friends. I could have called him, I suppose, and pressed the issue, but I wasn't that forward, so I moved on. Was I in love with Brian at that point? I don't think I had spent enough time with him to be certain that I was in love with him. I just felt there was something that could be explored.

So I met Tom and found myself falling in love with him. I was twenty-seven when we got married. We dated for about two years and lived with each other for a month before our wedding. He proposed with great difficulty. This was a man with extremely cold feet. For sure, I pressed the issue. I was feeling the biological clock beginning to tick. I wanted to get married, and if Tom didn't want to get married, I needed to know so I could move on. When we finally started to try and make a baby, it took three and a half years for anything to happen. I was given fertility aids, and at thirty-three, I had twin girls.

Tom said he wanted to have a baby, but when it turned out that I had fertility problems and, upon testing, his sperm count was low, he became rather passive-aggressive. He was told not to masturbate so that when the time of the month came for me to possibly conceive, he could give it his best shot. Well, he began to masturbate six times a day, and he would tell me about it. He said it was his way of releasing stress. He admitted that although he wanted a baby, he would be just as happy, if not happier, if we remained just the two of us.

When I got pregnant, I guess he was happy, but he was more terrified. When the twins were born, he said that he was thrilled to have them, but he had very little to do with them. It was always about Tom's schedule and the way he wanted it, not about what the children needed and wanted. I took off about six months and then went back to work part-time, but even then, Tom didn't make one bit of effort to help me. I told him that if he didn't kick in, he would have no relationship with his children. It came to the point where I was working full-time and still doing all the child care. He felt that was completely and totally my job. He might have picked up a grocery item here and there, but he wouldn't pick up the kids from nursery school. Both have some learning disabilities, and homework often posed problems, but I was the one to deal with all that as well. Tom wouldn't even admit that the kids had these deficits. He didn't want to know anything.

I wanted a third child, and we ran into the same infertility issues. This time the doctor recommended artificial insemination, since we'd been trying for months and months and I was becoming anxious, and besides, I was that much older. We went through one artificial insemination, which was no big deal for Tom—all he had to do was whack off in the jar and I'd take it to the doctor's office. I didn't even ask him to come with me. The first time didn't take, and although I was disappointed, I hadn't really expected it on the first try. So, the next month I watched my cycle with great anticipation, and when the time was right, I gave Tom "the cup," and he looked at me and said, "I'm not doing it." He said it wasn't on his agenda—he didn't want a third child, and he dug in his heels. I was crying hysterically. I had gone through the entire month of hormone therapy once again and had my heart so totally set on cradling a new baby and raising another child. I even tried to convince Tom that maybe this time we'd have a boy. He refused, and the topic was never up for discussion again.

I counted my blessings with the girls. I was happy being a mother, but I was also frustrated that I didn't have a moment to myself. I wasn't happy with my marriage or with Tom. So why did I want another child? Partially because, as I looked to the future, the thought of having both my children out of the house at the same time was depressing. Part of me also thought maybe I'd have a boy this time, and Tom would have a son, and maybe that would change things. Looking back, I suppose I wasn't thinking clearly. Even in the beginning of our marriage, before the twins were born, Tom wasn't easy. There was a lot of passive-aggressive behavior, but I sort of let it slide. He had to do things the way *he* wanted to do them and until I got to the point where I would get totally hysterical and couldn't stand it anymore. When he did back down, it would be only for a short while—just long enough to get me calm and back to being the "good wife," and then his behavior would start all over again: He was demanding and obstinate and withholding and angry. As the years went on, Tom was angry more and more until it became all the time.

My parents have what seems like a storybook marriage. They never fought and even said that fighting in front of children was a horrible thing to do. So I was brought up with a distorted view of what a good marriage and a good relationship were. In my mind, having fights with Tom and hearing him yell at me meant that we didn't have a good marriage and that he didn't love me. I went out of my way to do whatever it was I had to do to make him happy, to placate him and smooth things over. I tried to make things as reasonable and quiet as possible—to my detriment. I was determined that we would have a good and wonderful life no matter what the cost was to me. My parents' marriage was the template for my marriage: working together, being together, holding hands after so many years. That was what I aspired to, and I thought I would have it. Unfortunately, their marriage was a tough act to follow, and a wife cannot create it alone.

When I had been married for about five years, right before I got pregnant with the twins, Brian called. He was in town, and we got together for an afternoon. We went to lunch and then to a park, and I realized that I could still lose my heart to this man. What I had felt initially was still there, and I was aware that I was increasingly unhappy with Tom. But Tom and I had a commitment, and I was already trying to conceive our child. Still, I wrote Brian a letter after that day, saying something like it was so good to

see him and I'd missed him and just because I was married, it didn't mean
that our relationship had to change. In other words, I left it open to interpret
any way he chose. At that point, I knew the writing was on the wall in my
marriage. And to be honest, I wanted a friendship with Brian, but I wanted
the sexual part, too. Had things been wonderful with Tom, I never would
have written that letter. I would have told myself this was something that
could have been, and even though I felt the attraction, I would have put it
behind me and squelched it.

After the twins were born, and after the second run of fertility treatments for the third child who never came to be, Brian's job was taking him
more and more often into New York City, so I saw him several times within
a shorter time span. Very quickly, I realized that I was falling in love with
him. It was the first time we'd had enough time to spend together, and it was
obvious that we were magnets for each other. When the twins were about
six, Brian and I started sleeping together for about a year. Tom became aware
that there was something more between Brian and me, although he certainly
didn't think there was a sexual aspect. He even gave me an ultimatum. He
said, "You either stop seeing him, or we end the marriage now." Of course,
I chose not to end my marriage. I had to tell Brian that I couldn't see him
anymore. And I didn't see him for quite a long time after that—maybe about
eight years. In the meantime, he got married. I was so jealous. He said that
his wife reminded him of me, and that really hurt. After he got married, he
fell off my radar screen.

Shortly after I stopped seeing Brian, I had a brief affair with another
man whom I had met through work many years before. We were clearly attracted to each other. We'd have dinner together on occasion. Tom wasn't
suspicious, and part of me wondered why. Perhaps he thought I wasn't particularly desirable. He made me feel taken for granted. Well, one night this
man and I discussed the fact that we were attracted to each other, and we
went back to his place.

We got together only about three or four times after that. I was terrified that Tom would find out. My husband and I had a reasonable sex life. The affair wasn't about sex, per se. It was that my marriage was quickly going downhill. Tom and I were fighting a great deal. I was still trying to make things happen between us in a positive way, because I wanted to be in a good marriage, and although I stated my needs clearly, they remained unmet. I needed to talk and have Tom hear what I was saying. I wanted more of a social life together as well as apart. I wasn't able to go out with friends because I wasn't allowed to get a babysitter; Tom said it was too costly, but he wouldn't stay with the kids. He was very controlling, especially with money. He looked at every single bill and said, "Don't spend, don't go, and what do you mean you won't be home for dinner tomorrow night?" He wasn't interested in getting together with other couples, so over the years, we started going out less and less. In the last few years, I've pushed Tom to go out and make friends on his own, because come the time when we are no longer together, this way I know he'll have friendships. I don't hate him. I don't want him to be miserable. I want him to have people around who care for him. But I cannot be the one, even now, to do everything emotionally for him. For years I felt like I was being held prisoner.

The other man, that brief affair made me feel very *pretty*. And he made me feel smart, and he listened to me. If I said "I'm feeling such and such," he echoed what I said and let me know that he was hearing me. In other words, he responded. I ended the affair when the man's marriage started to have problems. He was newly married, and I felt it was important for me to step away. Besides, we worked together, and I was becoming fearful that someone would find out. He took it just fine, and that was that. We saw each other from time to time within the context of our profession, and he was still flirtatious, but he was also clear that there were boundaries at that point and I was unwilling to cross them.

Just about that time, Brian called. He left a message on the machine saying he was in town. He was living in Chicago now. I hadn't heard from him in years. Actually, Tom picked up the message and said to call him back. He'd written down the number. Brian was no longer a threat to Tom. He'd been out of our lives long enough. I felt nothing for Brian at that point other than curiosity, to see where he was in his life. He came to our house one afternoon (Tom was at work and the kids were in school). I wouldn't have recognized him from Adam. He'd changed a great deal. We were sitting on the couch, and he was talking a blue streak. Months later, he told me how nervous he was because he was attracted to me. He said I'd gotten even better with age. So there we were talking and laughing, and it was just like old times but even better. We went into the kitchen to make some coffee, and I was sitting up on the counter waiting for it to brew when he came over to me and kissed me. We went from the kitchen back to the couch and then to the bedroom. We made love, and I remember thinking how good it was way back when and that it was even better now. We went out to lunch, and then we came back and made love again. It was the most wonderful day. Truly, at that point, I didn't think it would go anywhere else. I thought, Okay, this was a wonderful afternoon and great sex, although I was having a hard time convincing myself that was all I wanted. I couldn't let myself think that I was looking for a deeper relationship with Brian, one where I didn't have to beg and plead for love and affection and companionship. I also had to remind myself that Brian and I were both married to other people.

Brian called the next day and said he would be back in New York City shortly and could he see me again. I said yes. Gradually, I fell back in love with him, and the intensity and the power of this relationship just blew us both away. He made it clear that he wasn't looking to break up his marriage, but he asked how he could be married and have a child and be madly in love with me. Despite the fact that my marriage was poor, I felt exactly the same way. I thought, Oh my God, what do I do?

This all came at a time when I was trying to establish a life of my own.

The twins were no longer babies, and I had told Tom that he could stay with them when I went out with friends, since they were no longer infants who required a four-page instruction sheet. I promised I would leave their meals, so all Tom had to do was be with them. He didn't take my proclamation too well. He was not only upset that I wanted some independence, he was furious. It's taken years for him to accept that I won't give in anymore.

When I was with Brian, which wasn't more than once a month, I'd tell Tom that I was with friends. Once or twice, I said I was meeting Brian for dinner. Tom asked if anything was going on between us, and I reassured him and said it was just dinner. And I reminded him that dinner wasn't costing anything, so that was an added incentive for him. I was always home by around ten or ten-thirty, and Brian often drove me home. Neither Brian nor I was looking to shake up the status quo.

About a year into this newest phase of our affair, Brian and I went away for the weekend to a country inn in Vermont. I told Tom that I was going to a girlfriend's house in the Hamptons, and the girlfriend covered for me. Brian and I had the most glorious and romantic couple of days together. One morning we were sitting at a table having breakfast, and a woman asked if we were newlyweds: She said we looked so happy that we were glowing.

When I flew home from Burlington and Brian went off to Chicago, I wrote him this gut-wrenching letter about the beauty of what we had together. I stuffed it in the bottom of my dresser drawer when I came home— under layers and layers of scarves. The next morning I felt Tom's presence standing over me before I even opened my eyes. It was palpable. He said, "Get up. We need to talk. I know." He had looked through my drawers and found the letter. Apparently, this wasn't the first time he had looked through my things, but it was the first time he had come up with something. Tom called Brian and threatened that if he ever saw me or contacted me again, he would call Brian's wife. The strange thing is, Tom never threatened to leave me, and he never threatened to break up our marriage. My affair was,

I believe, symbolic of something that was out of his control, and Tom always had to be in control. I didn't see Brian for quite a while, but we still spoke all the time. We talked each other through this, and despite the threats that Tom made, Brian never abandoned me.

All that happened in April. In June, I fell apart. I couldn't handle anything anymore. I couldn't bear life with Tom. I called a counselor and went into therapy and I didn't talk to Brian. I told him that if he was in my life at all, I couldn't do the work I needed to do for myself and on myself. I told him that he needed to back off. Over the course of the next few months, he'd call and say that he was sorry he couldn't be there for me. He understood that I didn't want to speak to him, but he was thinking about me and would be there for me in any way that I needed or wanted him to be.

Eventually, I began putting myself back together. I came to understand why I was unhappy in my marriage. I understood that it was holding me back and not allowing me to grow. I came to realize that Tom didn't love me as a woman but rather viewed me as a possession, as chattel. As something to be controlled and to make his life easier. Tom went to marriage counseling with me, and we broached all these issues. At first he was unwilling to admit to or want to change anything. A lot of our therapy consisted of me crying and ranting and raving and saying that I was willing to move forward with him—that I would put in the work—but he had to meet me as an equal and not try to control me. I asked him to let me in on the monetary issues— the investments, the bills, the checkbook. Until then he had kept everything from me. I think I know most of it now, but I am certain I don't know all of it. Much of it he kept at the office.

I told Tom that every time I begged and pleaded for something in my marriage that didn't happen, it just chipped away at me. I kept losing more and more feeling for him. I told him that I was afraid I would never get the feelings back again, but he didn't believe me. He also believed that I would never leave him. Sex was becoming less frequent to the point where it was rare. I just didn't want to. When I ran out of excuses—a long period or a raging headache—I'd give in. That kind of rejection was difficult for him, considering that he is such a sexual creature. When we did have sex, I had to take myself someplace else in my head.

I had to admit to myself that I was still in love with Brian. After a time, I called him, and he planned another trip to New York City. Tom found out, or maybe he suspected, and he called Brian and told him not to dare see me again or he would call Brian's wife. In my mind, this was not the way a husband should behave with his wife. This was the way a father behaves with a daughter who's seeing someone he disapproves of. It was not born out of love or passion or even grief—it was born out of control. It was a power play. It was more like "Don't touch my stuff." Brian called and canceled his trip. He just said there was a lot of stuff going on at home and he wouldn't talk to me for a while. It made no sense to me. A few weeks later, he called and told me about Tom's phone call. I guess he wanted the dust to settle a bit before saying anything. I was furious. Whatever feelings I may have had left for Tom were gone. Just dead and buried. I wanted nothing to do with him.

After all that, Brian and I continued to see each other. Brian still said he wasn't going to leave his wife despite how he loved me. I was the one to back off. I wrote him a poem that said how upset I was and how awful this was for me because I wanted forever. He had a P.O. box, so I knew his wife wouldn't intercept it. I made it clear that I needed to regain my life. But while I was separating from Brian, I didn't become closer to Tom. A few months later, Brian came back to New York and said he couldn't live without me. Since then we've only gone forward. He comes to New York every three weeks now. We talk about the future. We talk about being together.

If, for some reason, things don't work out with Brian, I will still leave Tom. I worry about it financially, though. I worry about sending our kids to college, because we would then have to maintain two households. But I am not willing to live my life this way. I have no bond with Tom. I have no re-lationship with Tom. He's not my friend, and I need friendship. I need love and companionship. I don't have that with my husband. I think about how difficult it would be to be alone, but I am prepared. I know that when I leave Tom, he will become even more impossible, and all the anger that he's had inside all these years will explode. Although Tom has never hit me, I've been physically afraid of him lately. Recently, he got right in my face, and I did feel physically threatened. I pushed him away and he pushed me back and it blew my mind. The physical threat was there.

My relationship with Brian has allowed me to live my life in the present, perhaps with greater happiness than I would have had otherwise. In other words, I suspect that my marriage would have ended long ago if not for my affair with Brian. How strange a thought is it that an extramarital affair can keep a couple married? But you see, it makes the marriage tolerable. For whatever it's worth, it has allowed my daughters to keep their family intact. It has also secured a dual family income. But having Brian in my life has al-lowed me to leave alone some of the issues that I would have gone head-to-head over with Tom only to find, as I already know, that I might as well hit my head against a brick wall. I have chosen my battles differently. When I have more peaceful times, I utilize the hours to improve myself and grow stronger within myself. But the cost for all this has been great. It has cost me tears and loneliness and the reality that closeness and companionship did not, cannot, and will not exist within my marriage.

I'll see Brian next week. He'll be in town for a few days. I worry about Tom hiring a private investigator sometimes and having me followed. Or just finding out that I'm still seeing Brian. My girlfriends keep telling me to be careful. I am careful. But I want forever with Brian.

MRS. D

&

Mrs. D is an extremely expressive, brutally honest forty-four-year-old mother of three children from a suburb of Miami. She has been married for twenty years. She has lived many lives and continues to live with a duality that is known only to her. In every other way, she is a typical suburban wife, active on the PTA and currently in the midst of taking her daughter to visit colleges. She is also a recovering alcoholic and drug addict and was once a prostitute. When she works, she's in sales, and Mrs. D could sell snow to the Eskimos. She is witty, warm, charming, and although she has an air of tragedy around her, she faces life with abandon and an almost eerie courage. Her search is for kindness—something she finds quite often in strangers. By her own admission, she simply wants to have fun. Is she looking for love? More likely, it's comfort and attention that she's looking for, and perhaps in all the wrong places.

My first marriage lasted about five minutes. I eloped one night with a Frenchman, Jean-Paul, to Las Vegas, simply because we had nothing better to do. We were probably together for six months and then divorced. I was living in L.A. when I met him. He was an Adonis. I met him just after my life had spiraled out of control; he swept me off my feet at a time in my life when I was an absolute mess. Thank God I'm not with him now. During the six or seven months when I was—and I was only twenty-two at the time—I had been in some serious trouble. I knew the marriage was over in that chapel in Vegas. And that was very much what my life was like back then: just crazy. That marriage is a blip in my life.

Before I met Jean-Paul, I was living an extremely illegal lifestyle and had gotten seriously into drugs and alcohol. I never finished college and got into a street life. I had an extremely untended childhood. When I was very young, not even a teenager, I was able to do whatever I wanted. I've been looking back on it for the last few years, and it's all so clear in my mind: I was drawn to bad people. Some of them were good people who had *turned* bad because they were also allowed to do whatever they wanted, and no one watched them or told them not to because they could get hurt. It got so bad that I was even abducted by a gang, and the police and my family were looking for me. When I finally got away from those people, I moved back in with my family, but that was no real solution.

A couple of years after I left Jean-Paul, I married my current husband, Nick. I was twenty-four. I was never in love with Nick, either. I *love* him, but I never was *in love* with him. This is a tough one. I suppose I should define what kind of love I'm talking about. Is there a special definition for this certain kind of love?

I'm a recovering alcoholic and just celebrated one year sober. My husband is a two-week recovering alcoholic and keeps falling off the wagon. If you asked me two weeks ago how my marriage is, I would have told you that I just met with a lawyer and was about to throw Nick out. But then Nick hit rock bottom, and now he's in recovery and he's trying.

Look, I've never had any ideals about marriage. I had never seen a good marriage when I was growing up. I never *aspired* to have a good marriage, but I wanted children desperately. In between Jean-Paul and Nick, I dated doctors and lawyers, but there was a little bit of "I don't feel good enough about myself" and "They really don't know who I am" that tainted those relationships and ruined any potential they might have had. Those men courted me, and there were opportunities with them, but the moment they got serious, I had this feeling that I would be found out for who I really was. Even now who I appear to be is not at all who I am. As far as those doctors and lawyers were concerned, the only real part of me that they knew was the kindness and humor, but the part of me they didn't know was questionable, and I didn't want to answer any questions.

Nick was, and still is, one of the kindest people I've ever met in my life. Did he bowl me over? No. He was *kind* to me. He was *available* to me. And I have never had anyone in my life—the important people who shape our lives, like mother, father, sister, brother—who was available to me. Nick comes from a big Greek family. They weren't intellectuals, and I thought that was good. They didn't probe me too deeply. Nick still doesn't know the extent of the life I led. He doesn't know that I ever engaged in prostitution. Nick was extremely accepting of me, but he's also a blocker. He didn't *want* to know. I don't usually tell anyone about my life, which is why I can tell this here, because no one knows who I am. I've also just gone through a year—for the first time since I was nine years old—sober, and I think that this is a way of clearing out and venting. I never accepted who I was before, and now I am working extremely hard at accepting myself and understanding how I got to be where I am. I think I've been denying who I am for my entire life.

Nick and I had our first child just months after we were married. In fact, the pregnancy is why we got married. There I was, not wanting to get married and pregnant anyway, so we went to the justice of the peace and moved to this suburb where we live now. We had a boy. And now he's about to be a freshman at Penn, and I am so proud of him. I also have a sixteen-year-old daughter and a fourteen-year-old daughter. I am a wonderful mother in a lot of ways. I have never told my children that I used drugs or alcohol as a young person, but they are well aware that I've been in A.A. To some extent,

I know they have a feeling that "Mom knows what it's like out there, she's been there, so don't go there," even though I have never really said anything. They *know*.

Last night I was trying to remember my first affair. The first time I had intercourse outside my marriage was fairly soon after I was married. I was at a birthday party for a friend, and my husband stayed home with the kids. I got drunk and was making out with this young kid. He was probably around twenty-two. Most of the time when I fooled around, I was drunk. I never had a guilt thing when I fooled around. I never wanted to hurt my husband, either. My one fear was that he would find out and *be* hurt. It all goes back to the same thing: I never went into my marriage thinking it would be the kind with a picket fence. But I did want kids, and I wanted a certain kind of life for them. I wanted to fit in and look right. I've never felt that I fit into any category. With Nick and the kids, I wanted us to be a suburban family, but I never really cared about being a suburban wife. I think that Nick probably knows that I "step out." As I said before, he blocks. And don't forget, until a couple of weeks ago, he was drunk.

Up until about a year ago, Nick and I had lots of sex. But to be perfectly honest, despite that, when I went out with my friends to a bar, I would end up making out with somebody. The minute you put drinks into me, I was out there and not really choosy. Sometimes I felt like the passionate part of me was dormant when I was in the mommy/suburban-wife mode. I needed that passion. I wanted it. And honestly, Nick never did it for me.

This past summer, I went on Match.com, and within a minute I saw a cute guy's picture, so I e-mailed him: I said, "I don't like to type my feelings." So we got on the phone. It was a rainy night in July, and I told him that I wasn't comfortable talking. My husband wasn't coming home from wherever until three or four in the morning anyway (he was drinking back then), and my kids were at camp. I told the guy I was coming over. Unfortunately, I have no fear of dying and no fear of dangerous situations. That's never gone away. I wanted to see this guy and I figured then we'd fuck. I always play the "I haven't kissed anyone but my husband in twenty years" routine—you know, men are like babies, and you have to say "You're my first."

Well, I went to this guy's house—he didn't live far from me—and had two days of the most incredible sex. I'd come home at five in the morning to change and then go back the next afternoon. It was the most fun I've had since the last time I had fun. He had been separated from his wife. He probably had a drinking problem, too. I walked in, and it was craziness. He was a very bright guy, but when I think back on those two days, I think he was probably insane. You know, he probably wasn't the best kisser, but it was still incredible. He was saying some weird things now that I think about it. And then I told him that I had to leave early that morning because my husband and I were going to see the kids on camp visiting day.

I had never done anything quite like *that* before. Why wasn't I worried that I could get myself killed? I have a tremendous faith. It just didn't feel like it was my time. The guy even said, after our tenth hour together, "You really shouldn't do stuff like this. Are you crazy?" I told him that I can take care of myself.

There were others. Some were months of make-out sessions. One guy was about twenty-eight. He was just a few years ago . . . Oh God, I keep remembering more men. But understand, I was drunk. I was insane.

I had an incident recently with another guy I met on Match.com. We went to a local bar—and this was since I'd stopped drinking—and I told him that the man sitting next to him was my daughter's best friend's father (he and his wife are divorced) and the bartender was a friend of my son's. But the guy didn't care; he was all over me. I kept telling him that I *knew* people there, but in all honesty, that was also part of the fun for me. I wondered why I was putting myself in that position, and it frightened me. I suppose that I was frightened partially because I was sober. I hear this is quite common after you stop drinking. I mean, I was sober and I didn't know if I could even kiss someone without alcohol. I didn't know that I could feel passion without alcohol. I drank my entire life. The feeling of this man being so in my space aroused me, and I was just thanking God that I was alive and that I could still feel passionate without alcohol. A few days later, I ran into the woman whose ex saw me at the bar, and she said not to worry, that he wouldn't say anything. I suppose I was a bit fearful, but I had started taking steps to leave my husband, because I felt that our marriage was the wrong model for the children.

I have tried to be a loving wife and mother, but I don't think human beings are meant to live devoid of passion. I think we all need to feel that we're erotic and touchable and special. It was only in the early stages of our marriage that my husband was demonstrative and touchy-feely and passionate. The times that we had sex, we were drunk. We both liked sex, but I was always the aggressor. Now, understand, you don't have to be passionate to have sex. I equate passion with kissing and touching and looking into someone's eyes and grabbing their belt buckle or putting your hand on their back or their thigh—my husband does none of those things. My husband is not passionate. I used to tell my husband early on that all he had to do was kiss me on the back of the neck when I was emptying the dishwasher and I'd be his. Nick was very mechanical. His attitude was "If we're going to touch, it's because we're going to have sex," and he was giving me a signal. There was nothing in between—none of the playing just to be erotic and sensual. I see this trait in his family. My sisters-in-law feel the same way about Nick's brothers. The whole family is a bunch of cold fish. Nick and I were pretty experimental when we were drunk, and I really taught him the ropes. But with alcohol, I can be with a one-legged blind man and it would be good.

One time I met a guy at a company Christmas party. I had gone to the party with the chairman of the board, and I was drunk and dancing and left the chairman for this other guy who wasn't even part of the party—he was someone's guest. We got in his car, and I opened the glove compartment to get a cigarette or whatever, and there was this big gun. He was, like, a wiseguy. We went to some bar and got wasted, and I can't remember whether I slept with him or not. No, wait, I did. He said he was divorced, and I assume he was telling the truth. He was one of these tough guys, you know? We were making out like crazy at a restaurant after we left the party. I saw him for a while after that. We'd go to a hotel in my area. As I usually did with a new guy, I went through my little speech about my flat chest, and he just whipped the silicone pads out of my bra, threw them across the room, and we had amazing sex. He was funny as hell and had a lot of money. He was just *fun*.

Nick doesn't care where I am when I'm out. That first night I spent with the wiseguy, I told Nick that I was sleeping at a girlfriend's house. The kids were little. They were sleeping. But now, as I hear myself say this, it's so obvious that Nick didn't *want* to know.

Is there a duality to my life? Some people will say there is, but I will tell you why I never question a duality in my life. And it may sound like a crock of whatever . . . I knew when I was getting married, it was to have children, and that was the only reason. What I do is irrelevant to what kind of wife I am and what kind of mother I am. This is who I am. I am honest with my husband without being mean. I don't think that you marry someone in order to reshape them. He is who he is. This is why I will never and have never gone to marriage counseling, because we are who we are. Neither of us will ever change.

Do I do these things, and did I do these things, because I don't feel good about myself? Absolutely not. I did them because I like them. I do them because I like them. I'm sorry to be so crude, but I like the feeling of a tongue down my throat. When someone holds me and tickles me and we giggle, I like it. It has nothing to do with love. I know my husband loves me to the best of his ability. But there is a very big difference, and there always has been, between the other men in my life and my life with my husband. I imagine that eventually, we'll get divorced. We're still living together and we're good friends. We even had sex the other night—whoop-di-do. Do I think I will stay with him? No.

Could I ever be in a monogamous relationship? I could, but it's not important to me. I don't really care about monogamy. I could fall in love with someone, though. I really think I could. I love Nick. I really love him. But if I was ever to be monogamous, the guy would have to be funny, passionate, not mean. And above all, kind. Do I strive to fall in love with someone? No. I have this core of reality that other people might find depressing. I thank God for the fact that I have known physical passion. I may have been a slut—wish I could think of a nicer word—in high school, but you know what? It was fun. Oh my God, it was fun.

I never think about how my lifestyle will unfold as I get older. I think part of what makes me who I am has nothing to do with age. I have a passion for life. It's not that I love life. I'm not one of those people who wakes up every day and jumps for joy, but I have a passion when it comes to my physicality, and I think it will transcend age and time and will always keep me feeling vital.

As for my daughters, I would feel very sad for them if their life turned out like mine is now. They love their father very much, yet they've asked me what I was thinking when I married him. It's not a malicious statement. Their clarity is touching. They see the passion and humor in me. We have lots of fun, my children and I. We laugh and listen to music and giggle. Their father is not that much fun. They see me try to cajole Nick and try to be silly with him and jump on his lap, and they see that he doesn't respond. In some ways, I think my daughters feel bad for me.

What makes me sad about my life—this makes me get so emotional—is that I had a very painful upbringing. I don't like to sound like a drama queen; I wasn't beaten physically, but I was so neglected. It was as if I wasn't there. I was allowed to do everything because I was ignored. Everyone in my life responded to me except my parents.

At the moment, I am seeing an older man. I always thought that maybe I could be an Anna Nicole Smith type. He's seventy and divorced. I don't want him to touch me, though. I'm not ready. I go with him on his boat on the weekends. He's quite wealthy and has offered me the world, but I can barely look at him, and he annoys me. He's grumpy. He's not nice to people. I told him that Nick and I are trying to stay together, but he doesn't care. I keep seeing him because he has money. I figure if I get divorced and need money, here's this guy who's throwing himself at me. But I can't get to the point where I can let him touch me. I'm trying to be pragmatic about this guy, but I can't, because physically, he makes me sick. So I'm learning a lesson from this: I sure can't do it sober. I guess I'm just not quite the same old hooker I used to be.

I suppose, in a way, my childhood and my marriage are reflections of each other because there is an element of neglect in both. I still get to do what I want whenever I want to. Nick gives me freedom along with the benign neglect I'm accustomed to. It's bittersweet, but it's what I am accustomed to having—or perhaps not having.

MRS. E

⚐

Mrs. E is a warm, bright, lively, beautiful fifty-four-year-old woman. The mother of four children, she is an English teacher in a Chicago suburb and has been married for thirty-one years. To the suburban community where she and her family live, Mrs. E is a shining star and, of course, a mentor to many young children. Her husband, Peter, a local real estate lawyer, appears to be a loving husband, a real family man, and a pillar of the community as well. Mrs. E is the last person on earth one would think would have an affair. All seems perfect behind the white picket fence and in front of the blackboard— but it's not. She is deeply in love with another man. It's not that her husband isn't loving; Mrs. E's conflict lies in the fact that it's difficult to forsake a husband whom she loves with the devotion of a sister to a brother.

I never understood how women, working women with husbands and children, could have affairs, because I never understood how they could fit them into their schedules. I remember when I smoked—I always found enough money to buy cigarettes. I've come to realize that it's the same kind of thing when it comes to having an affair.

Sam, my lover, is married. Not happily, though. Of course, a cynic would say that men say that all the time about their marriages when they're having affairs, but in my case, it's true. He's not happy. As for me, my God, I never thought I would have an affair. Neither Sam nor I exactly fit the stereotype for people who would do this, but then again, I guess there really is no stereotype. Of course, before I started this affair, I thought there was.

Sam and I live in the same town, and oddly, we'd never run into each other before That Fateful Day. We also work in the same town. I have kids and he doesn't, so that could be one reason why our paths never crossed. Well, one day we met on the train coming home from work. Remember that movie with Meryl Streep and Robert De Niro? It's called *Falling in Love.* They meet on a train as well. I only recently saw the film . . . amazing how art imitates life. Anyway, Sam and I talked and started to become friends. We are *still* very good friends. We share many interests. I'm a teacher, and he's an editor of children's textbooks at a small publishing house that I never knew existed, so right from the beginning, there was a lot to talk about. And we still talk a great deal. Our relationship evolved from a very fundamental, connected friendship.

One day we decided to meet for lunch. One lunch led to another and then to another, but it was always just lunch. It did get to the point where we started getting together with our spouses on the weekends. That stopped rather abruptly when we confessed to one another that we were planning those evenings because we missed each other on the weekends. The weekend evenings were never an obvious ruse to either his wife or my husband, but they were becoming worrisome for us. I don't want anything to be obvious. And it's not that our spouses are oblivious; it's more that the two of us are extremely discreet.

The first time we four got together, I told my husband, Peter, that I had become friendly with this man I met on the train, and my husband thought nothing of it. Now, another husband, a different type of man, might have said something like "What the hell do you mean? You met some guy on the train, and now you're bringing him home?" But I suppose that's another example of the lack of passion in my husband and within the realm of my marriage. You see, I have been very angry at my husband for many years now. I don't understand why he doesn't want intimacy. It's not as if we live in a culture that doesn't have a million ways to teach yourself how to do something like have sex. We've never even had a screaming match over this, because we don't fight—and that's a lack of passion as well.

As for Sam and me, neither of us wants to hurt anybody. Our affair just happened slowly, over time, and as I said, it grew out of friendship. The first time Sam and I were alone together was in a hotel in Chicago. I was absolutely terrified. We were both quite nervous. We both had legitimate business there for a few days—I had union meetings, and he had editorial meetings with some bigwigs from New York City, so it worked out perfectly. Funny, because in the beginning, you don't know what you're getting yourself into. When we were just friends, we shared a common value that neither of us would ever cheat on our spouses. We had this morality. We both had a sense of true commitment. It was like that tenet became our mantra, and we kept saying it over and over again. After a lunch when I drank too much wine, we began to talk more about the possibilities of each other—and that was six months later, after riding on the train together every morning and meeting for lunch maybe once a week or twice a month. We were friends first. But maybe we kept reciting our mantra because we were either trying to convince ourselves or each other, or because we had a sense of what was coming.

The hotel in Chicago was not the best. As a matter of fact, it was sort of seedy. We knew it wasn't great, and it was off the beaten path, but we didn't know how seedy it was going to be. When I think back to that, I laugh, because the place where we go every week now is like the joke motel in the town where we work: People often talk about it and say that they have day rates and call it things like "Happy Hour Hotel." It was a world I once knew nothing about, and here I am going there every week.

I remember that first pivotal lunch when we knew it was more than lunch. Nothing happened that was earth-shattering except that I was eating a salad and had something on my cheek, and he reached across the table and brushed it aside, and it was electricity for me. It was such an intimate act that it scared me. It all came together. We admitted to feeling, without saying it aloud, a connection. Something happened that was different, and we stopped fighting it. We'd had too much to drink, and I told him that I had to walk off the wine to perform properly at my presentation in front of the principal later that afternoon, so we started walking. It was snowing like crazy. I looked at him and asked, "Where are we going?" He laughed and said, "Down the street." I said, "No, I mean personally, where are we going?" We stopped, and he looked at me and said, "I don't know. Probably in the wrong direction." That was the only time we were indiscreet. We stopped in this town where we both work, and he kissed me for the first time, and I felt like I was eighteen. It was pretty incredible. I went back to the school and had the meeting with the principal (after lots of coffee), and then I met Sam at the train that evening, and on the ride home, we just talked.

Surprisingly, I have never felt guilty. Maybe it's rationalization on my part, but I really do love him, and it's been very difficult. In the beginning, when we were falling in love, it was such a strange feeling, because I thought, This can't be happening. I really felt that it was impossible. I'd been married for too long. I never thought about falling in love with someone else, and I never thought about falling in love again and certainly not while I was still married.

My husband and I really have very little in common. We have the kids, of course, and that's a very important part of both of our lives. But the kids are grown now. None of them lives at home anymore. My husband and I have been through counseling. The bottom line is, we live like brother and sister, except we never fight. We haven't had sex in three years. I know that my husband feels guilty about that, but he doesn't know how to fix it. He doesn't even attempt to have sex with me anymore. At some point he did, and I swear, I never rejected him. I wouldn't reject him even now. Another wife might wonder what he's doing for sex, but I don't wonder, because I think he's just not doing anything. It's a performance issue with him. He's not comfortable having sex. Having sex was okay when we were trying to conceive our children, because there was a purpose to it—it was procreation, not recreation. He's really lousy at sex, and I think he knows that, that's why I don't think he wants to do anything about it.

If Peter wonders what I do for sex, well, he's never asked. I asked him a few weeks ago if he wondered about me, and he said, with a shrug, that he hadn't given it much thought, and then he changed the subject. It's like he thinks if he doesn't ask, then it's not an issue. As long as I'm there and right beside him, which is ultimately what he wants, then he sees everything as fine.

I still see Sam every day on the train, but for the last four years, we meet once a week at a motel. It's not a standing date. We fit it into our schedules, but it's every single week. We go to the same place every time, and he signs a different name every time. It's one of those places where you can drive up to the door so no one ever sees me when I come in. We can't stay there very long—maybe an hour at the most—because we have to get back to our jobs. But we have lunch a lot. People see us at lunch together, but I don't think they suspect there's anything more between us than a friendship. We look like such unlikely candidates. Of course, I could be fooling myself, but I don't think so. I'm always talking about my husband and family to my friends and my colleagues, and the truth is, my husband and family are a very important part of my life. People don't suspect me.

Sam and I rationalize what we're doing by saying that, well, you see, we're keeping each other married. That sounds weird, doesn't it? You see, neither of us was happy until we met, and now our marriages are more bearable because we have each other. By the way, his wife is awful. She is the most self-centered, egotistical person I have ever met in my life. I think the reason he hasn't left her yet, regardless of me, is that he was so determined to make his marriage work, since he married late in life and the idea of failing at marriage really bothers him. He's coming close to leaving her. We really try not to talk about our married relationships too much, though.

Sam satisfies me and gives me things to look forward to—the conversations, the lunches, not just the once-a-week at the motel. And I miss him terribly when I'm not with him. He's away with his wife right now, and I don't think they're having sex, although he's honest with me and tells me that they do have sex every once in a while. When he tells me that they've had sex, I get really jealous. It drives me crazy. I think that's part of the reason this all might come to a head a little bit sooner, because it's beginning to drive him crazy, too—that I'm upset and also that he feels an obligation to have sex with her every so often.

People who know Peter and me—our friends, neighbors, colleagues—all think we have a wonderful marriage. We still sleep in the same room, you know. I tell you something, if we do end up getting divorced, it will be the biggest shock to everybody. Recently, I gave Peter an ultimatum: If he doesn't start sleeping with me by the time our oldest son returns from overseas in six months, then we have to separate. And the thing is, I guess it's an unfair ultimatum, because what if he does? Then what do I do? Although I think my ultimatum is unfair, I've been married for so long that I would probably stay with him if suddenly we began to sleep together. I suppose that sounds awful, but you have to understand that despite the fact that I'm in love with someone else, if Peter and I could have something of a real life together, I would stay. Not breaking up my family is of the utmost importance to me. Besides, despite my affair with Sam, I made a commitment to Peter a long time ago, and the weird thing is, I believe in that commitment.

If I leave Peter, it won't be *because* of Sam. I'd want to be alone for a while if I left my husband. I wouldn't just jump into something else. I was married so young. Time alone is something I've never had. I was right out of college when Peter and I were married. Why did I marry him? My father had died, and I thought I had found my father in my husband. I don't think Peter gets the idea behind romance in marriage. For him, marriage was and is about providing things. It's never been about passion. Even in our youth, as I said before, our sex life was poor. Our conversations were strained, and yet I looked past it, perhaps because we had children so quickly. The kids were always a viable excuse for not having sex and conversation—I mean, when you have little kids, it's exhausting. But when the kids get older, what's the excuse? Well, there is no excuse. We're not having sex, because we're just *not*. But even though sex with my husband was never great, I loved him so very much. I still love him. I think he's a wonderful man. He's been a wonderful husband from a practical point of view, and a devoted father, but the marriage is just so dead. There was never any passion. What scares me to death about growing old with him is boredom. I would die inside. I would wither away. The thought of retiring with him—I can't do that. I would work until I took my last breath.

I worry a great deal about how the kids would react if I left Peter. I really think the three older children would blame me, and that scares me to death. It's another reason why I would never leave Peter and dive into a relationship with Sam. If I did that, I would lose all my children for sure, and they're my main concern. Another man in my life would have to be an eventuality. My children are the reason I have stayed with Peter all these years.

Don't think for a moment that I've had an unhappy life, because I haven't. When you're raising children and working, you're involved in a million different things. You don't really have time to stop and think about anything. You're going from one activity to another. Your life revolves around the kids, the jobs, the kids' activities, the school. Peter and I were always with people who were doing all the same things that we were doing.

Our circle of friends, after all these years, has seen only one couple divorce, which is so weird, because so many of the marriages are not happy. The reason for the divorce was infidelity: The husband had another woman.

As far as being in my fifties and looking ahead to my sixties with another man, I don't want much. I'm not looking for extravagance or a lofty lifestyle. I simply want someone to have dinner with in a restaurant, someone with whom I can share intelligent conversation without pregnant pauses. I want to feel comfortable. And then I would love to go home and have sex with that person. At this point in my life, I realize that I have emotional and intellectual needs and that sex is a very important part of a relationship for me. Sam awakened so much of this in me. For years, I thought that when it came to sex, I was just dead.

I would never tell Peter that I was having an affair. I would never want to hurt him. He would be devastated, and yet I also think it wouldn't come as too great a surprise. He would think that he deserved it, in a way. Peter has no idea, and I don't think he realizes that I am as passionate as I am. He doesn't see me that way because I've never been that way with him. I tried in the past, but I stopped trying quite a while ago, because what he doesn't know about women is incredible. At this point, I'm angry. I don't have a big ego, but why isn't he worshiping me at this point in our lives? I believe that my husband likes women but doesn't see them as sexual beings.

Peter and I have been discussing our marriage and have gone to therapy several times over the last twelve years, but there's no mind connection anymore, there's no body connection. We're no longer going—I think both of us realize it's pointless. Our therapist loved Peter. And I loved Peter. I still love Peter. Our therapist would look at me and laugh because she understood how I loved him. One time she asked me to leave the room so she could talk with Peter alone, and when she called me back in, she said that Peter had something important to tell me. Well, I was really waiting for the walls to come down, and he looked at me and said, "I just don't know how to pleasure you. I'm sorry." That was it. The big revelation. I was speechless, because he just stated it so matter-of-factly. It was an apology. Clearly, he wasn't planning to do anything about it. Peter and I do things and go about our lives with each other in a rote fashion. There was never a crisis or a sharp turning point when we disconnected. It was all gradual. The problem is that my husband is incapable of passion, and it's hard to abandon someone who's incapable. It's a sad situation, because otherwise we might have had a wonderful life together.

Sam thinks my husband is nuts. He can't understand how Peter cannot feel passionately toward me. If I found out that my husband was having an affair, I'd be relieved. It would at least give me an explanation—it would give me something I could fight for. It would give us some passion.

If I knew, positively and unequivocally, that my husband and my kids would be all right, I'd leave. But I am so afraid of what would happen to my kids and to Peter. I feel that if I left him, it would take the life out of him. As I said, he's like a very dear brother to me, but that doesn't make for a good marriage. It's tragic, really. He's so many wonderful things, but he is not what I need in a man. He is not what I need in a husband. You see, the thing is, if we walked down a beach together, we wouldn't hold hands. There would be nothing. And we do walk on the beach. And sometimes at night, if we walk on the beach, I suppose that sometimes we *will* hold hands, but the way friends do. He won't kiss me. Sometimes I have the feeling that Peter is waiting for cues from me, but at this juncture, I'm just out of cues.

There are days when I say to myself, Why doesn't Peter just *die?* Isn't that awful? And it's not that I really mean it, and then I get so angry at myself for even thinking it. But for me, I suppose that would be the easy way out. Then I could mourn him and not be judged or forsaken by everyone around me. They say to be careful what you wish for, don't they? More often I wish he would run off and meet someone as dull as he is. I actually have a friend who would be absolutely perfect for him. They know each other quite well, but they're both too dense to see their compatibility. I suppose the way I feel sometimes is that I wish Peter would just vanish. It's also gotten to the point where there are weeks that I am such a bitch. I won't talk to him or I'll be obnoxious and I think, Well, maybe now he'll leave me. But he wouldn't leave me—not in a million years. It's like a dog, when the owner beats it, and the dog remains loyal to the owner in spite of the cruelty.

My husband is thrown by so many things, whereas Sam embraces things, and he embraces what he knows and doesn't know and wants to learn. Nothing throws him and nothing shocks him. I think my husband has always been the way he is, and the older he gets, the more set in his ways he becomes. It's increasingly difficult to get through. I asked him one day what he wanted to do when he retired, and he looked at me and said he doesn't plan on retiring. I asked him why, and he said because he'd have nothing to do.

Yet in some ways, Peter is a rock for me. He's predictable and reliable. If I had to go through a crisis, he'd be there for me. When I have gone through a crisis in the past, he was wonderful. I know he would still be. I suppose if I were chronically ill, my marriage might be perfect.

There are women in my community who would call me a selfish bitch if they knew that I had this other man in my life. They would think I was horrible, but they don't know what goes on—or rather doesn't go on—at home. I would guess that there are probably a lot of women out there who don't care about passion, either—they have their husband, house, and kids and don't care if their husbands screw whomever they want, providing they still have their "stuff." Well, I don't feel that way.

I've come to realize there is a passion in me that's hard to extinguish. I felt it when I was in my twenties, and I suppose that sometimes it wanes a bit after we have kids, but then it comes back—or maybe it's that we learn to suppress it. Perhaps it gets displaced and misplaced—we have babies and juggle marriage and career. Back in our twenties and thirties, when we were having babies and had little kids, we were tired. Maybe some women also equate sex with the possibility of pregnancy. But then we get into our forties, and the kids are off and running, and that's when we need the foundation of our marriage. Now, in my fifties, I realize the passion in me is still there, or rather, it's finally been ignited.

The older I get, the more I realize that if I could spend just two years in absolute bliss, it would be worth it. And I suppose that somewhere in the back of my mind, I think about the fact that my husband might take me back if it didn't work out on the other end.

If I make this decision to leave my husband, it won't be either *about* or *for* Sam. It's only going to be about me. The thought that plagues me is that I'm leaving behind the devil I know for a devil I don't know. And I don't know how I would feel if I severed my marriage. I don't know whether or not I would feel compelled to still care for Peter. I do believe that if I severed the marriage, within six months Peter would be with someone else. And I'd be happy for him. He's a good person. He deserves to have somebody who loves him and somebody who's wonderful. I love him, but not in the way I would like to or should. He needs to find someone who's on the same wavelength. He needs companionship. I don't think Peter's particularly unhappy, not the way I am. On occasion, I've confronted him. Here's a typical scenario: I say it's evident that we're not happy together, and he says, "Fine, then let's get a divorce," and I look at him and ask him how he can throw away thirty years of marriage just like that, and he says because if we're not happy and it's not working, then that's what we should do. It's the easy way out for Peter, although I don't think he really means it or realizes the ramifications of divorce. He just flees from confrontation.

I'd be surprised if my husband and I are together a year from now. Then I think about the kids coming home for holidays and I don't know that I could leave. I can't think about Christmas and Thanksgiving and things like that without our family together. I just don't know the answers now.

You asked me what would happen if I came home one night and Peter had something special planned for me, a romantic setting and a nice dinner. He tells me that he will do anything to make me happy because he loves me and doesn't want to lose me. He asks me to tell him how to love and pleasure me and promises that he will listen. How would I feel? That would be the fairy tale. That makes me cry. You see, if I had my choice, I wouldn't be in this position. I wish I could have a happy, healthy marriage with Peter. But I also don't regret this other relationship for even a minute, because it makes me feel alive and has done so much to enrich my life.

MRS. F

Mrs. F, forty-eight, is the mother of two children. A child advocate, she has been married for fifteen years and lives outside of Dallas. Mrs. F places her own children above all else, and she describes herself as a devoted and loyal wife—of course, loyalty is quite different, she says, from fidelity. She is unhappy in her marriage; she and her husband have no intimacy and no conversation. She has been having an off-and-on affair for the last four years with a man she has known for a lifetime. This man has always held the key to her heart. Although she wrestles with the fear that this affair could potentially harm the structure of her family, for the first time since she was seventeen, she is following her heart.

Dylan is someone I've known and loved in many ways since I was seventeen. I suppose it was an affair of the heart long before it became physical. We maintained our relationship even when other friendships came and went within our group. He was a bit of a rebel. He had a very unhappy family life, and he traveled a lot to get away from everything after he graduated. People were always angry with him because he didn't keep in touch, but that wasn't who he was. He was in and out of people's lives, including mine, but I always took extra care to stay in touch with him, and I knew he always appreciated that. I knew that behind the tough-guy veneer, he really needed to keep connections—his friends, including me, were the only family he had. There was always something special between us.

He's had a history of coming and going, and I was always so sad when he left and I never knew when I'd see him again. Now, of course, his free-spirited ways are even more painful. When I was in high school and then college, my boyfriend didn't have a problem with the friendship that Dylan and I shared, because he understood it was pure friendship. It made me happy to keep the connection with Dylan even when it was sporadic. It somehow nurtured my soul. He sent letters and postcards from all over the country and all over the world. I have old phone books that trace his history on the road. Imagine, I've known him for thirty years now, but the last four years have been profoundly different.

I guess when we were about twenty, he came back home for a while, and this time he had a girlfriend. My boyfriend, Bobby, and I were planning to take a year abroad, and Dylan and his girlfriend came with us. We all had this wanderlust, and I can't believe my parents even let me go, but we did. It was all so crazy. We went to London and then to Paris, and although we took courses here and there, it was hardly like we were enrolled in college. Bobby and Dylan bought motorcycles. It was incredible. I ended up going overseas with Dylan a week ahead of the others: His girlfriend didn't have her passport in order, and Bobby screwed up somehow, so his plane ticket was for the week after ours. Dylan and I spent a week touring around and stopped in all these little towns and drank wine and ate exotic foods and just had a great time. We were going to all get a place together, but we ended up staying in youth hostels until the last three months, when we got a little flat in London before we headed back to the States. After we got back to the States, our lives took different paths. I broke up with Bobby, and Dylan and his girlfriend broke up, but the four of us still remained friends. And we've all remained in touch over the years—aside from Dylan, we three are all married with children.

When I was about twenty-eight, I met Steve, the man who would become my husband. Dylan lived nearby then, and I introduced Steve and Dylan, and they actually liked each other. It was important to me that the two
of them got along. I think Steve was intrigued by Dylan, and Dylan thought
Steve was a nice, decent guy. Steve did say to me at one point, after spending
an evening with Dylan and me, that he really felt awkward and as though he
didn't know where he fit in with the two of us. It was a good year when Dylan lived close by—we'd get together with old friends quite a bit, and Steve
joined in as well.

Then Steve and I got married, and Dylan took off again, yet there was
still a sweetness between Dylan and me. I always told Dylan that I thought
he was such a sweet man, and he would argue that he wasn't, really, but admitted that he was with me because I was different. There were times I'd be
driving in the car after I was married and certain music would come on the
radio and it reminded me of Dylan and my heart would pause and I would
have such a sense of him and I would miss him. It was a real visceral feeling;
I felt a loss when he wasn't around. Yet I still didn't entertain the thought
that I was in love with him. I loved him, but it was just different. To tell you
the truth, I don't know what I thought it was when it came to him.

Steve and I had known each other under a year when we got married. I
really wanted to get married and I really wanted to have children. I remember reading this article that said a thirty-year-old woman had a better chance
of being captured by terrorists than finding a husband—maybe that's not
such a high odd anymore, but back in the 1980s, it wasn't a great thing to
read. Friends of mine were married and a lot of them had babies. I wanted
the same. Steve and I were happy. We lived in the city and had great jobs
and money. Life was easy. Part of me didn't want to look at what wasn't
right with our relationship. I knew that Steve wasn't the grand passion of
my life. I knew it when we were together and engaged and even at the altar,
but I thought, Well, all the hearts and flowers and passion and fairy tales

aren't really what love is about. I thought, You make a life and you make a commitment to marriage and you make love happen. It was hard for me to put aside that desire and the belief in happily-ever-after, but I did because I wanted the trappings of marriage. Since I was a young girl, I'd been always caught up in the romance and the love and the idea of a soul mate, and I figured those were just youthful fantasies.

Like Dylan, Steve comes from a broken home and an unhappy family. As inane as this sounds, Steve was very nice to me. He was kind. He wanted to be with me, and he wanted to marry me. Was he really in love with me? I don't think that was quite it. I think he was looking for a family, and I come from a large, close-knit family. I think he wanted a lot of the same things that I did, like children and a home, and I think I provided stability for him. I had good friends and a good job and a good head on my shoulders, and in many ways, I took care of him and he needed that. He didn't take quite as good care of me. There were things I saw in the beginning of our relationship that have become more pronounced throughout our marriage that are not right.

The main thing was that Steve's and my sex life was not satisfying, not even in the beginning. At least that's the way it felt to me. I always loved having sex. I loved the intimacy of it and the physical aspect of it. I loved the reveling afterward. He was self-conscious and inexperienced. I didn't care that he seemed inexperienced or immature sexually, because I thought if you're with someone, and you love someone, then you grow together. His reticence and self-consciousness disturbed me, though. He enjoyed sex in the way that a teenage boy enjoys sex, not a man who's about to get married. But I thought I could fix him. I was very adept at looking at the good aspects of our relationship and pushing aside the things that weren't good. In other words, I did what I can do all too well: I looked the other way.

Even after we were married, I still had hopes that I could fix our sex life and get him to relax and loosen up. It wasn't like we weren't having sex, it was just that it was lousy. Sex with him started making me feel uncomfortable and self-conscious, and that was something I never dreamed could happen to me. I think that's what bothered me most of all, because it just wasn't me. Shortly after we were married, I found a stack of pornographic magazines on the shelf in Steve's closet. It humiliated me because I wanted to have all this physical intimacy and excitement and games with him, and he seemed unable to, and yet he had these magazines. I was shocked. I addressed it with him, and he was totally embarrassed. He had no explanation. He was as flustered as a boy. He said, "I won't do it anymore," as though he were a child. I tried to explain to him that I didn't have a problem with the magazines if they could be an extension of a good healthy sex life between us. I felt that they were in lieu of our sex life. They were like weird competition. I would have even been willing to experiment with him with movies and magazines and whatever, but we had no basis for that. We didn't have that kind of sex life or intimacy. The one time I recall having really good sex was after my brother's wedding. We drank too much, and all of Steve's inhibitions were down.

I got pregnant about three years after we were married. Even throughout that pregnancy and right up until the end, I initiated sex. And then we had the baby and all hell broke loose. I was so in love with that baby and so involved with that baby. Of course, I was overwhelmed, because I was a new mother and I was exhausted. I'd stopped working, and we had moved to the suburbs about a month before the baby was born. For better or worse, I admit that the baby took over our lives. The baby also became a good way for me to avoid having sex with Steve because sex was so unsatisfying and I was so exhausted anyway at that point, it hardly was worth it. It had gotten to the point that sex was so bad that afterward I would be depressed for days because I felt like a receptacle, not a lover. We still had sex—it was just with even less frequency than before I had the baby.

After a while, I began to get angry. A lot of Steve's guy friends would ask him to come into the city on the weekend, and most of them were still single. There I was looking for romance, and Steve would come home late, reeking of booze, and the whole scenario made me feel hurt and angry and sad. I never drank as a teenager, and I never drank as a young adult, except for at my brother's wedding, and then I probably had only a glass or two of champagne. I'm a pretty cheap date. My family never drank. Steve's drinking just hit me in all the wrong places. When we were dating, he drank socially, and heavily at times—that's what he and his whole group did. I never liked it, but now we had a baby, and it really upset me. Once we made our move to the suburbs, he seemed to spend more and more time with his friends, both after work and on the weekends.

I was so taken with the baby. I admit that I probably excluded Steve to some degree. I liked only what I did with the baby and how I managed the baby. Looking back, it wasn't the right way to be, but I guess it's what happens more often than not with a first child. It wasn't like Steve didn't love the baby or want to hold him, it was that I was so anxious. My son wasn't a good sleeper. Because he was so fussy, it became easier for Steve to hand him to me and say, "He wants *you*." I would walk the floors all night long with the baby, and Steve would say, "Well, I can't help you because I have to get up for work in the morning." I felt very passionately about my role as a mother, and I really wanted to get it right. I remember in the beginning when the baby was born. The first day that Steve went back to work, I thought I would have the baby sleeping and I'd have dinner on the table. It was right out of *Ozzie & Harriet*. Steve came home and I hadn't managed to get out of my pajamas. I don't think I even got to brush my teeth. I was such a mess. The baby had been crying all day. He was colicky. I was sitting in a chair holding the baby when Steve walked in, and Steve took one look at me and I'll never forget the look on his face. He looked at me with such disdain. He walked away from me. I felt so horrible. He had completely dismissed me. I felt like a failure on all counts—as a wife, a mother, and as a lover.

After that, I always felt a chasm between the two of us. Steve was working, and I was home, and it was like he was saying, "What's wrong with you?" Of course, he was earning the money. Until I had the baby, I had been working at a large public relations firm and making more money than Steve. I was so hurt and angry. When we were both working and coming home at the same time, we divided the chores and cooking. Suddenly, because I was home, there was no more division of labor. He helped me with nothing. What got to me then—and still does—is the notion that yes, he was working outside the home all day, but I was working inside the home. And why didn't he, and why doesn't he, want to spend time with the kids? How can a father not want to get right in there and be with those kids? They're such wonders. I resented that Steve did not seem to be able to bask in our family. At the time I didn't consider that he was jealous. Looking back, I think he probably was. I think he still is jealous of the children.

About three years later, I had another baby. I conceived our daughter the second time that Steve and I had good sex! Our son was about two, and Steve and I decided that we should have "dates" on the weekend where we'd put the baby to sleep and make a nice meal and open a bottle of wine and make love. It was a plan. The first three weekends, Steve stood me up. He managed to do something else. He'd go down to the city and hang out with his friends and come back stinking of beer, which I detested. We were really fighting at this point. I was so hurt. But the fourth weekend, I had been out for the evening. It was the first time I had been out at night since the baby was born. It was a beautiful warm spring night, and I went home, and I guess I was feeling pretty good about myself. Before I had left that evening, Steve had said that we would try our date again the following weekend, and he sort of apologized. Well, I decided I didn't want to wait for the planned date on Saturday night, and we made love and it was nice. That night might have been the last time it felt that way. After that, we had sex only when Steve made it obvious that he needed to get laid. It was juvenile. There was nothing loving about it. Foreplay consisted of him making himself and his needs clear in this sort of puerile and almost joking way. There certainly was no romance. And I would still talk to him about it and try to make the effort. He either couldn't get it or wouldn't get it. To this day, it baffles me. Every time I tried to talk to him about our sex life, he just shut down. I felt so rejected and so undesirable. I felt unattractive and old.

During that time when Steve was running around, I called Dylan and told him how I was feeling. The last time I saw Dylan was before my son was born, and I remembered what he said to me as we said goodbye. He said I was always the one and only constant in his life. I'll never forget that. So, I was talking to Dylan one Saturday night when Steve was out, and Dylan could tell I wasn't happy about it. Dylan asked, "Why is Steve out with friends when he could be home making love to you?" And I thought, Yup, that's the question. It's those kinds of things that Dylan and I were always able to talk about.

I could never bring up the topic of why with Steve. It remains an unresolved conversation. I know that Steve won't understand my anger, and frankly, I think I'm afraid to tell him, to hurt his feelings; basically, I am just not that confrontational. As for the sexual relationship that I don't have with Steve, I am beginning to think that he didn't and doesn't want the love-making. Steve and I have not made love in five years. We sleep in the same bed, but we don't touch. He faces one way and I face the other. And he doesn't want to talk about it. At this point, I don't *want* to make love to him. I love him because he's my husband and the father of my children, but sexually, I want nothing to do with him. We have no spiritual or intellectual connection. As much as we are sharing this life, we have nothing in common but the children and the bills.

About four years ago, Dylan came to visit. I hadn't seen him in about five years at that point, though we had spent a great deal of time on the phone. He was settled in Wyoming, and we spoke a few times a month. It was always fun. We always connected. We always laughed, and I could talk to him about anything and everything. One of the things I started talking to him about was my marriage. He was living with a woman and seemed happy. But Dylan had a history of discarding people. I was the only one he hadn't discarded, because I wouldn't allow it. The funny thing about Dylan is that I knew him well enough, and I know him well enough, to know that he doesn't extend himself emotionally to people, and that was always okay by me. One time I was talking to him when I was very upset about Steve, and he couldn't talk to me because he was at work, and he said he would call me back. I figured he wouldn't call me back for weeks. I had no expectations. Anyway, about an hour later, he called. Now, I know this sounds like a silly thing to think, but it struck me, because it was so out of character for him to extend himself. We talked, and then not long after that, our conversations got somehow more flirtatious, not even necessarily directed at each other but just in the way that we talked about relationships we'd had and our own relationship. It became a little edgier, and there was a spark of something that hadn't been there before. And then, as foolish as it sounds, I started thinking about him at night as I fell asleep, and I started to dream about him. One day we were talking, and we both realized that we had been thinking about each other in a different way. Over the next year, we spoke at least every other day. It was something I looked forward to, and it became very romantic and loving. There was suddenly this flood of emotion. We had always said "I love you," but now it had a different meaning, because there was a sexuality attached to it. The thought of—not necessarily the doing. It was more like a fantasy. We would say, "Okay, if we're not with someone when we're seventy, we'll end up together." It was kind of that old "What if?"

Well, that fateful weekend, Steve was out of town, and Dylan stayed at the house. It was clear that Dylan and I wanted to spend the night together. It was the most perfect day. The weather was beautiful and the kids were great and he played with them and the kids loved him. I put the kids to sleep, and Dylan I had dinner and drank wine and talked and listened to music and laughed and laughed. We talked about everything. I told him I loved him in every way and had always loved him in every way at different times in my life. He kissed my hand and looked at me and looked so happy. And then he kissed me, and it was just unbelievable to me. I had thought about it for so long. I was overwhelmed with the entire evening. Then he told me how much he loved me and how deeply he felt for me. I was so overwhelmed I could barely respond. Here I was with this man I'd loved for so long, whom I had always thought of as my soul mate. It's hard to imagine sometimes having what you want, and this was all such a surprise for me that I didn't know what to do with all my emotion. We made love for hours—until the morning. And then I had to get up and get the children to school. He left, and it was very hard for him to leave and hard for me to let him go. We didn't know quite what to make of everything. I asked him if we had just ruined everything, and he said he didn't think so.

As the day wore on, I had so many other emotions. I felt guilty. I felt I had betrayed my children and that somehow I had ruined their lives because I was about to fuck up my marriage. As far as my relationship with Dylan, I was panic-stricken that I would be relegated to the long list of women he had slept with. When he got back to Wyoming, we spoke and said that we missed each other. His relationship with his live-in lady fell apart, and they broke up. Then, true to my fear, our relationship started to change. He wasn't as available to me, and he wasn't as warm. I felt he was keeping me at arm's length, and it just tore me up. I had a choice: I could get angry and push him away or be who I was, and that was someone who loved him. I remained as constant to him as I always had been, but I was still very hurt. I realized that he was and is the love of my life. I also knew that I couldn't ride off with him into the sunset. I am devoted to my husband. I have a strong sense of family and what my children need, and I put them first. For better or worse, my children come before me. I also knew who Dylan was: He'd never been married, and he didn't want kids, and as great as he had been with my kids, I knew that was just one day. I tried to get rid of my illusions, and it took a couple of years. There were times over those two years that he would call and be warm and close and other times when I felt I was at arm's length again. There was never any question in my mind that I wanted to stay in his life, and despite his obvious wrestling with his emotions for me, it was apparent that he wanted me in his life as well. It took a lot of nurturing to get our friendship back to where it was before we made love. There is no question that making love changed us.

He came to town last week. I met him in Dallas. He stayed over at a hotel, and I spent the night with him. Oddly, it was Steve's suggestion—he thought it would be foolish for me to drive home late at night, and he's always known how important Dylan is in my life.

I wondered if anything could be as magical as it was four years ago. I suppose in some ways I am not very proud of myself, but it's amazing the lengths we will go to when we feel love and passion for someone. I couldn't wait to make love with Dylan again, and it was better and closer and more intimate than it had been four years ago. The thing that worried me was that there might be an awkwardness about us now that wasn't there the first time, but there wasn't. For sure, the dynamic has changed. We need to redefine who we are to each other. We're older now. We talked about who we will be to each other as the years go on. I would love to think that at some point in my life, when the kids are grown, we will spend the rest of our lives together and grow old together.

MRS. G

⚘

Mrs. G is a forty-five-year-old bundle of energy. She's been married for fourteen years, and although she and her husband are now separated, they still live under the same roof for the sake of appearances. She is still in love with her husband. Both are professors, living in the South, and her husband is nearly twenty years older than she. By her own admission, she cheated for revenge. She justifies and explains her affair by saying that her husband's infidelity sent her into the arms of another man. Now she wants to reunite with her husband.

When I met my husband, I fell in love with him instantly. It was love at first sight. He was a suave, nice-looking man with a great body. He dressed very well and always had on a beautiful outfit. A classy guy. He was previously married with children. In fact, his daughter was just a few years younger than me. We had a great relationship in the beginning, although fitting into his family, with his kids, was difficult.

We had a huge society wedding and enjoyed a great beginning to a new life together. We had a child, and things really seemed to be going well for about six years. Then I started to discover some things about him that I hadn't noticed when we dated or during the early years of the marriage. I had some instincts about a few things, but I couldn't be sure.

He started to go on lots of golf trips with his buddies. This was something new. I was always invited to go, and sometimes I went, but I felt uncomfortable because the other guys rarely took their mates with them, so I stopped going on the trips altogether. I totally trusted my husband and knew that he enjoyed these trips with the boys. I enjoyed the time I had with him, and I enjoyed the times I had alone when he traveled. My husband comes from a well-known society family, and he and his father were in all of the society groups and so on. I assumed the trips and the times away were part of the whole society thing. For me, I fell into his social crowd even though my upbringing had been markedly different. I felt as though I had it all. Boy, was I mistaken.

One night my girlfriend called me. It was summer, and she'd just gotten a new car, a convertible, and wanted to take me for a ride. My husband hadn't gotten home from work yet, so I said, "Why not?" We drove around the neighborhood because I wanted to stay close to home, and I wanted to be close by when my husband got home. For some reason, I especially missed him that day. We drove around and around, nearly in circles, and as we drove past a certain house, I told her to stop the car. My husband's car was in the driveway of the darkened house. My girlfriend said, "No way, he's still working." Looking back on that day now, I realize my "friend" knew something all along. Anyway, I practically forced her to stop and back up so I could look closely at the plates. It *was* his car. I was furious. I knew all of my husband's friends. Who was this person? My friend came with me as I ran to the front door. She tried to stop me, but I rang the bell. She begged me not to, insisting there had to be a rational explanation. When no one answered, I banged on the door and yelled, "Open up!" Still no one came to the door. I was nearly screaming at that point. It felt like an eternity, and finally, a tall, attractive woman opened the door. In fact, she was beautiful. In some ways I thought she looked like a more statuesque and slimmer version of me. She had an attitude as she asked what I wanted. I answered by saying

I wanted to know where my husband was, since his car was parked in her driveway. When I said that I was his wife, she slammed the door in my face. I stood there in shock and was even more shocked when my husband came to the door with no shoes on. He asked me what my problem was and said he was just helping a friend who needed something done in the house.

I asked, "What are you doing here without your shoes on? You look mighty comfortable to me."

"She's a coworker and needed me to help her do something," he explained. "We were just relaxing."

Well, at this point I was livid and quite loud, I must admit. Someone called the cops, and when they arrived, I was still screaming. "You're cheating on me! We have a child. Why are you doing this to me?"

The cops took me away and arrested me for disorderly conduct. I was later released. When I got home, my husband had the nerve to say that I had embarrassed him, and he wanted to know why was I hanging out with the woman I was with in the convertible. He said that she was no good. A bad influence. I was speechless, considering that I'd had to go to the police station because he was cheating on me. None of it made any sense.

Needless to say, the relationship was permanently scarred, and although we reconciled through counseling, it was never the same. I loved him, but I was damaged for life. I wanted to stay with him for my son's sake, but I felt that all bets were off at that point—and I was going to have some fun, too. I didn't need any more damn marriage counseling. Hell, I decided that I needed a man who was going treat me right!

During our counseling sessions, when I asked my husband what had happened in our marriage, he said that he was bored. That he needed excitement and the other woman provided that for him. I was devastated. I'd been satisfied sexually in the marriage and never intended to cheat, but after hearing his confession, cheating was the only way I felt I could retaliate. And I wanted to retaliate.

Men had always come on to me, but I had never responded. I was in love with my husband, and until he cheated on me, I never would have considered being unfaithful. I knew that I was acting emotionally and not thinking clearly, but my husband took a lot from me. I had been so devoted to him, and his infidelity sent me into shock.

I was going to do something for myself, no matter what the cost—that was the night my friends and I went to a club in our area. I wasn't looking for anyone in particular, but I was on the prowl. There were so many good-looking men, and they were all staring at me. I was really feeling good, but I wasn't ready to meet someone and sleep with him. I was just enjoying the attention.

I met a guy there. A judge. He was so nice and seemed to just want to have a conversation. We talked until almost five in the morning. He gave me his card and I gave him mine. I figured I could move this along at my own pace. The next day he called my office bright and early and asked me to dinner. I knew something could happen, but I still wasn't ready to cheat on my husband. I convinced myself that it was just dinner. I kept telling myself that I loved my husband and wanted to get back with him, although it wasn't the time yet, because he had hurt me.

I went to dinner with the judge. I looked good. Had my hair done, bought a new dress. He had just separated from his wife and said that he simply wanted some female company. Although I was nervous, I felt confident.

We had so much fun at dinner. He told funny stories and talked mostly about himself, and I laughed and smiled. We stayed at the restaurant pretty late. Afterward, we went for a drive, and just drove around aimlessly. He took me back to my car and said to call him when I got home. I didn't call. The next week there were flowers at my office and a note asking me to dinner again. Shortly after the flowers arrived, he called and asked why I hadn't called him that night.

"I've been thinking about you a lot," he said softly. "Let me know what you want to do. If you don't want to see me, let me know, but I really want to see you."

He was so charming. He wanted to have a quick drink that night, but I said it wasn't a good idea. Although the next night, I gave in.

I knew what I wanted to do. I just kept putting it off. Things with my husband were bad. I tried over and over again to have sex with him, but he refused. We were sleeping in the same bed every night, but there was no sex, no romance, no nothing.

I had dinner with the judge a second time. We went on a short cruise in our town, and while we were there, he kissed me. He asked me to come home with him, and I didn't protest. He understood that I couldn't stay overnight, and he promised to get me home early. I had sex with him without an ounce of guilt. It was great. I felt needed and wanted. He'd arranged for a car service to get me home that night, but I didn't go. I stayed all night.

The truth is, I'd lied to my husband and said I was staying that night with a friend. I knew I was going to screw the judge. I felt pretty bad about lying to my husband, but I didn't feel bad about making love to that man, not at that point, anyway. I mean, I wouldn't have cheated on my husband if he hadn't cheated on me. I needed to have a man make love to me. Although I tried to convince myself that I no longer was in love with my husband, I look back and doubt that was true.

I have cheated seven or eight times since then, and to this day, I still love my husband. I just kept looking for someone to love me.

The passion has left our marriage. He chose to cheat, which drove me to cheat. He provided our family with a great lifestyle. We lived in a great house in a great neighborhood. We still haven't divorced, although we will never get back together in the way that a marriage should be. We have what's called a live-in separation. I suppose that I like the prestige of being married and saying I am someone's wife. I mean, I am forty-five. Who wants to say they aren't married at forty-five? I am still living the life of a wife, although I'm miserable. I want him back, but he doesn't want me anymore. Our "marriage" is purely for public appearance: We still live together, and I sleep around when I want to. I suppose he does, too.

For me, well, I stay in the marriage for love, stuff, and history.

Mrs. H

Mrs. H is in her late fifties and lives in Virginia. Everyone thought that she would marry young, but she chose to focus on her career. She enjoyed sex and dated many men, but no one was interested in marriage. She dated successful businessmen, professionals, and even a well-known musician. In her late forties, she met a sincere, hardworking man, and she married for the first time at forty-eight. She felt it was imperative that she be married at that point in her life. Her family was pressuring her mercilessly. She felt that a man—any man at that point—would make her life complete. She wasn't happy being by herself. Her loneliness and insecurity were becoming increasingly difficult to hide from the men she was dating. Her prospective husband's work history wasn't particularly stable—he had changed jobs several times—but he always managed to be employed, and he was a nice man and a good companion. Then he developed a degenerative disease and became an invalid.

M y sexual history was an open book to everyone who knew me. I made no secret of the fact that I enjoyed sex. In a word, I suppose I was loose: I met a man, and if I liked him well enough, I'd end up in bed with him. It's just that I felt very good and confident about my sex life. I felt that I was able to both give and receive pleasure. The problem was, I couldn't find the right guy to marry me, and that became an obsession.

I had a great childhood, despite the fact that my parents died when I was a little girl. I was raised by my aunt, who was pretty loose herself and always had lots of men around. I had sex for the first time when I was twelve, and I really fulfilled a lot of my sexual dreams and desires during my early years. I went to a community college and chose to live at home with my aunt because it was so free and easy. I could have sex at home. My aunt and I had an understanding that we could have men sleep over as long as they didn't stay more than two nights, and we didn't go after each other's lovers.

After college, I worked my way up at a local computer company, was promoted quickly, and became a vice president by the time I was thirty-two. I was meeting and dating a lot of guys, but none of them wanted to commit. I was being satisfied sexually but couldn't meet someone to marry. Of course, back in my thirties, I felt that I still had time to meet someone and marry. My goal was to make as much money as I could at a young age so that once I got married, I wouldn't have to worry about finances and I could have a baby right away. All of my friends were married and had kids. It was starting to bother me, and I envied them, but I was a career woman. I thought that kids would be for later in life.

After I turned forty, and after many affairs with married and single men, I started to stress out because I felt that I should have been married. The clock was ticking. I'd dated a very famous singer, an actor, and a multi-millionaire. I had sex with them in all sort of places, but they would not commit. They all left me to marry other women. There was almost a superstitious aspect to me as well—I felt guilty about the affairs I'd had with married men and swore I would never do it again if I could just find someone who would marry me. I remained a confident person, but the fact that no one wanted to marry me was beginning to make me feel desperate. I would have done almost anything to get married. Not being married made me feel incomplete. As long as a prospective mate had some type of job and was honest, I would have married him. My criteria were narrowing rapidly. I wondered if I hadn't compromised my chances for marriage by putting my career first. I began to think that I'd made a huge mistake.

Late in my forties, I finally met a guy. He was handsome, previously married, and ready to get married again. We dated for six months, and I must have asked him to marry me. We got the ring, eloped, and had a civil ceremony at the county courthouse.

He and I both knew that he couldn't contribute much financially, but I had earned and saved enough for us, providing he could pay some of his own bills. I was fine with our arrangement. After all, I was finally married. He had been living in a small rental apartment, and after we were married, he moved into my suburban home. He enjoyed sex as much as I did. He was almost sixty, and although his sexual energy was fading, with the help of enhancement drugs, we were active. We also enjoyed each other's company. Children were not a part of the picture. His children were grown, so we got a chance to have an adult marriage and relationship. It was nice. I actually grew to love him, because he made the effort to make our marriage fun.

We remained happy for several years, and then one day he came home and announced that he had been diagnosed with a rare and degenerative disease. The outlook was good, but the doctor warned us that he would have to stop taking Viagra until his medical treatments ended. The doctor also warned that my husband's sex drive was going to wane, and worse, he wasn't sure when it would return.

I was traveling abroad a lot for work. Our marriage had settled into a fairly normal and comfortable state. I didn't like being away from my husband much, since he was ill, but I had little choice, since I was the breadwinner. I tried to make my trips as brief as possible. By then I was only fifty-something and still had a voracious sexual appetite, and no longer with the worry of becoming pregnant. I'd adjusted to the fact that I would never have children, after working through those issues with my therapist. I was finally free, finally married, and my husband's condition was deteriorating.

He was becoming markedly weak, slow, and almost unable to move around. We hadn't had sex for quite some time, but I had grown to care for this man, and I didn't want him to suffer. Suddenly, the doctor's original prognosis wasn't quite as optimistic. The treatment that had promised to at least assuage his condition was no longer a viable alternative.

I promised myself that I was going to make my husband happy through what now appeared to be the last few years of his life. It was devastating. I didn't want to do anything to hurt him, but I wanted to have sex with someone. I wondered if it would be wrong to have sex with a man just for physical pleasure, since my husband was no longer able to have sex with me. I didn't want to leave him. I wanted to love and take care of him. I asked two people for advice, one of whom is a close friend and the other who is my therapist. Both had different opinions. One approved and one didn't—and I didn't know what to do.

One night I met a single guy at a party who was not interested in marriage. I told him my story, and he seemed eager to please me, although he was a bit reluctant in the beginning, because I was married. He was handsome and in very good shape. I figured I'd make him an offer he couldn't refuse: to have sex with me on a regular basis without a commitment. I explained that my husband was ill and I needed physical companionship. I made it clear that I had no intention of getting divorced and was interested purely in physical satisfaction. I insisted that this was to be an arrangement, and there had to be rules. Perhaps that sounds cold, but the most important thing for me was to protect my husband and my marriage.

Other than the lack of sexuality, there was nothing wrong with my marriage at that point. We spent lots of time together, we had all of our meals together, and we went to the movies when he felt up to it. As his condition has deteriorated, the quality of the time we spend together has not lessened.

Sex with my lover is comforting. It isn't as good as it was with my husband, but it's satisfying nonetheless. Having a lover enabled me to release the physical tension I felt as a result of my work, as well as the stress of taking care of my sick husband. Now that I think back on it, my husband was a hell of a lover, but then maybe I'm confused and fantasizing a bit about our marriage.

My extramarital relationship has been going on for three years and has also evolved into a good friendship. He respects me for taking good care of my husband and taking care of myself as well. He once said he wished he'd married me because he appreciates someone who cares so much for her mate. He knows how long I wanted to marry the right man and how important it is for me to stay married.

I like my life, although it's not what I imagined it would be. I'm in my late fifties. Sex with my lover is less frequent, but there's a comfort because I know he cares about me in a certain way. I never would have dreamed that life would turn out this way, but I am happy to have two men in my life whom I adore and who adore me.

I often wonder if my husband suspects that I am having sex with someone else. If he does, he must be certain that I still love him. Sometimes I think there's a silent acquiescence on his part. He gives me a very warm kiss at night before we go to sleep in the same bed. We are still in love. And I know he wishes he could satisfy me sexually.

I have made a happy life for myself that is comfortable, and I don't feel guilty about my extramarital affair. I am truly happy. After all, I am still married, and that's what I always wanted.

Been There, Done That

Temptation

It seems that once you've had an affair, it's all too tempting to have another, especially if you've managed to get away with it. The affair is like a drug of sorts. You tell yourself it's not a good thing. It's risky. But the high was so sweet, so intoxicating. For some, as with any addiction, there is a determination to stay away. For others, resistance proves too difficult, and it's easy to find excuses.

There is wisdom and self-knowledge among the women in this category. Some recall their affairs without regret, still reveling in the magic of the moment; many continue to battle the pull of temptation to try it just one more time, recognizing that they escaped unscathed before and wondering if they can get away with it again. Then there are those who weren't planning to experiment, who were seduced—though acquiescent—but feel that an affair was not the answer.

A lot of personal history came out among the women who had been there and done that. Unlike the women who were still in the throes of the affair, this group appeared to be more reflective and forthcoming about their own self-esteem and the roots of their psychological and sexual needs—many of which were steeped in parental attachment and the way boys had treated them in their formative years. They were able to more objectively address their needs to nurture and be nurtured. The older women could go right to the heart of the matter with resignation and acceptance of themselves and their husbands. Two of the younger women left their husbands to be with their lovers, and so far, they have the happily-ever-after that they sought while they cheated.

From Mrs. K: "Sometimes my husband will mention the fact that we have no romance, but he always mentions it in an offhand way. To really get to the bottom of it, we'd have to talk about what happened, and I don't think he wants to—and I'm not willing to lie to make him feel better."

From Mrs. L: "How do I feel about women who cheat on their husbands? I think that sex is private. It's none of my business. I am the last person to judge."

Mrs. I

After four children and eighteen years of marriage, Mrs. I and her
husband divorced three years ago. She is now one of the few whose
story has a happy ending. At fifty-three, she is living with her lover,
John. She is happy, fulfilled, at peace, and has returned to school for
her MBA. Fortunately, income and finances are not pivotal issues
for her: Her husband left her financially well situated. Her children
never questioned the end of their parents' marriage. Mrs. I is beautiful,
highly educated, well read, and has a zest for living. She is also an
exemplary mother and a pillar of the community. The secret life she led
for the six years prior to her divorce was excruciatingly painful—not
so much because she was hiding the affairs but because her marriage
was laced with loneliness and distance. To her suburban Boston
community, however, her life appeared nearly idyllic.

I was thirty-one when I married Calvin, and although it was my first
marriage, I'd had several other long relationships. When I was nineteen,
I had my first love. I was still in college, and we lived together for nearly
six years. He would tell everyone that we were married, and although we
weren't married legally, it truly felt that way. Strange, I can't really remember what broke it up, and lately, I've often wondered. I think it was a
combination of the fact that he had a lot of issues and I didn't want to be

tied down. Basically, I think we broke up because our sex life started to deteriorate.

After that, I moved to Manhattan and took a job as a manager for a large import company. That was when I met Calvin. We were introduced by mutual friends just as I was ending another relationship. Calvin seemed nice, and he was very cute. We dated, and then about six months later, he asked me to marry him. He was preparing to move to Dallas for his residency in neurosurgery, and he wanted me to go with him. The truth is, it wasn't the first time he'd asked me to marry him—he'd asked after just a few dates, but I didn't take it seriously. (It wasn't until much later in my life with him that I discovered he had a history of doing that sort of thing—asking women to marry him after just a few dates.) So, although I didn't know him very well, I said yes. I can't remember if I was madly in love with him. He certainly was different from anyone I'd ever known before. He wasn't all over me, for one thing. I had to chase *him* instead. He was quite restrained—in retrospect, that behavior was foreshadowing. He also enjoyed the fact that I was successful and independent.

So we got married and moved to Dallas, and I knew early on that I had made a mistake. The problem was, I never felt that he appreciated me. I always tried to please him. And it wasn't that he was particularly demanding; it was just that he was totally immersed in his work. In the evening, I cooked beautiful dinners and served him, and when the time came for me to clean up, he wouldn't let me because the noise of the pots and pans clanging disturbed him. I catered to him and left the dirty dishes until morning.

We didn't stay long in Dallas. Calvin was disenchanted with the program. Additionally, he wasn't terribly diplomatic and had difficulty relating to others. At the same time that Calvin decided to leave the program, I was pregnant with our first child, our daughter. This was about seven months into our marriage, and it was an unplanned pregnancy. Sometimes I look back and think that if I hadn't had her and then the other three kids, I wouldn't have stayed married as long as I did.

Calvin managed to get a fellowship and another residency in Seattle, so when I was thirty-five weeks pregnant, in the middle of winter, we moved. And then, with an infant, we moved again to Chicago, where Calvin did yet another residency. Six months later, I became pregnant again, and it was unplanned again. It was evident that my children were keeping my marriage together. I loved being a mother. Calvin couldn't have cared less about the babies. He was focused only on himself.

When Calvin came home at night, we talked—about his work. We'd have dinner, and as soon as he finished his meal, he'd go to work on his computer. There was no interaction with the children. When the second baby was just two, I had another unplanned pregnancy and cried throughout the whole pregnancy. When the new baby was five weeks old, we moved to the suburbs of Boston, where we live now. Looking back, I realize we always moved when I was either pregnant or nursing or had an infant or a toddler or both, and I always made the move without Calvin, who would waltz in after we were ensconced. When we moved from Seattle to Chicago, I drove with two babies in a tiny little car. When I had to find us the home in the Boston area, I was pregnant again. I left the kids with my mother, located the house, negotiated the deal, flew back home, had the baby, and then flew back to Boston and closed on the house. And then I packed up the Chicago house and flew with three children to the new house, where the kids and I camped out (and I was nursing the infant) because the furniture hadn't come yet. Once we were set up, Calvin arrived. And then I set up his medical office. I would drop the two older kids at nursery school and take the baby with me. Within months, Calvin's practice was doing beautifully. And then I got pregnant *again*. It was so strange that I kept becoming accidentally pregnant, because Calvin was never interested in the sexual aspects of our marriage at all—that was a huge problem. Essentially, the four times we had sex, I got pregnant! Calvin didn't use protection, and I couldn't take the pill, and so it goes.

Calvin did not have a problem functioning sexually; he simply wasn't interested. After a while, it started to wear away at me. I went to a marriage counselor by myself, and then I made him go, but he said it was a complete waste of time and refused to continue. He acknowledged that he wasn't interested in sex but made no effort to change. He said he was tired. Of course, I took it very personally. I thought maybe it was the way I looked or the fact that I'd had so many children. He said it was neither of those things and really didn't want to explore the reasons for his lack of interest. He didn't make me feel inadequate as much he made me feel very unloved. He made me feel unattractive and undesirable. I was so unhappy with my life except for my children.

Months after the fourth child was born, I had an affair. I was asked to go on a business trip with someone with whom I used to work, an importer who needed help in Europe, which had been my area of expertise. I thought the trip would lift my spirits with a change of scenery. Well, I met an older man who began sort of courting me, and it felt so good to be desired. I was thirty-six and he was fifty-six. He was married, handsome in a way, but under other circumstances, I wouldn't have looked at him twice. I saw him a couple of times after that, when he came to the States, and it was terribly exciting. I wasn't in love with him and had no intention of even a long-term affair; I was just really needy. And he was good in bed—older and experienced. He came to my hometown, and we went to a seedy little motel nearby. My God, it was risky. I suppose if I'd had a husband who was more aware of me, he might have noticed that I was behaving completely differently— happy and smiling and relaxed—but Calvin was clueless. The affair lasted about six months, until my lover's wife heard him talking to me on the phone one day and all hell broke loose. She even discovered who I was and called and threatened to call my husband. I don't know if she ever called Calvin or not. Of course, when I spoke with her, I denied everything. I said there was a misunderstanding—that wasn't the nature of my relationship with her husband at all. It was only business.

A few years after that, I had an affair with a man in my community. Again, it was pure animal passion. I wasn't even remotely in love with him. I knew his wife rather distantly, and she found out about the affair and suspected it was me. Again, I denied it. I don't see either of them anymore. The whole thing was really sordid, and I have a lot of regrets about that one. It could have been quite destructive.

About six years ago, I became a devotee of e-mail. One of my correspondents was a very old friend, a man I'd known since childhood. We went to the same university, and over the years, we'd always kept in touch. In high school, he had a crush on me and followed me around quite a bit, although for me, he was simply the boy next door. Anyway, he was living in England, married with two children, and the marriage was most unhappy. I was planning a trip to England to see my grandmother, and he met me at the airport. I hadn't seen him in over twenty years. There he was, this graying middle-aged man, yet he looked the same to me. We fell right back into that old easy relationship. It felt so comfortable. We had lunch, that was all, and when I got back to the States, our e-mail relationship continued but became more intimate. We decided to meet again. The second meeting took a great deal of finagling and a lot of deviousness.

I knew I was going to have an affair with him. My marriage remained stagnant and lonely. All Calvin did was work, and looking back, I know now how depressed I was. My whole life consisted of doing things for Calvin and the kids. I was always doing busy work and constantly trying to distract myself. Maybe once a year, my husband and I would have sex. I even entertained the idea of having a fifth child. I knew it was the wrong thing to do, but I suppose I was afraid of the other kids growing up and leaving me alone. For some reason, I was unable to become pregnant, and now I thank goodness, because that would have delayed the process of separating and divorcing even longer.

I knew all along that I wouldn't grow old with Calvin. He wasn't interested in me. He was passionless. He was cold, although I can't say that he was unkind. He was superficial about anything that wasn't his work—when it came to his work, he was the best in his field. Sometimes I wonder if he was having an affair back then—I still don't know. Ultimately, it doesn't matter—maybe he was. At the time, I thought about it for a passing moment, but it had come to the point where I didn't really care.

I met my old friend, and we slept together for the first time. As I said, there was never any doubt in my mind that it would happen. We met in Lisbon, ostensibly on business, and spent five glorious days together. It was wonderful, and we were in love. It was also such passion. Unfortunately, it got to a point where he was careless at home, and his wife found out. Once again, I was named in the affair. He'd left a piece of paper on the printer—one of our e-mails. Really stupid, although sometimes I wonder if it wasn't subconsciously deliberate. Well, his wife went ballistic, and their marriage ended. It was primed to end anyway, but this was the catalyst.

We continued our affair. He flew here . . . I flew to Europe . . . and my husband knew nothing about anything. The thing is, even if my husband knew I had reconnected with an old friend, he simply had no interest in anything I did or anywhere I went—he never was curious about anything when it came to me. Despite the love affair with John, I had no intention of leaving my marriage. I thought that we should keep going not only for the children but also because I didn't want to give up my dreams. My parents had been divorced, and it caused tremendous problems for my siblings and me. I didn't want that for my kids. My parents didn't have a friendly divorce, and to this day my father will not acknowledge my mother's existence. I recall that he never paid attention to her. He was cold and unromantic and unaffectionate. I married someone as dispassionate as my father.

Well, one day Calvin announced that we should pack up the suburban house and move to Boston. He was making a ton of money, and he wanted to buy a Boston brownstone. I explained that it was out of the question, since the kids were almost through the school system in our town and I didn't want to uproot them. But Calvin was adamant: He had to live in Boston. I was equally adamant. I suggested we buy a pied-à-terre in Boston, but Calvin said no, he wanted to live in Boston all the time. Half joking, I said, "Fine, we'll stay here and you live in Boston, and we'll visit one another on weekends." "Well," he said coldly, "we might as well just separate." In the next breath, he said we might as well just divorce.

In some ways, I felt I was manipulating the situation. He was doing exactly what I wanted him to do. My entire sense of holding my family together went out the window when he said he wanted to live in Boston and would do so either with or without us. It was apparent that Calvin wasn't thinking at all about the children and the continuity of our family. I finally had to accept the fact that he was simply not interested in sustaining our marriage. We put our house on the market, and it sold rapidly. I found him a rather lavish apartment in Boston, and I bought a smaller house in our town. Of course, I was the one to settle Calvin into his new place. I'd hoped that if I set him up properly, he would become a better father to the kids. I thought they might actually spend time with him. I wanted the kids to be happy when they were with Calvin, and I wanted his place to become familiar. Not to mention that I had taken care of Calvin for eighteen years, and it was hard to stop. He was like my fifth child. As we were setting up his place, he said that doubtless he would have to remarry because he simply couldn't live by himself. I didn't respond, although it was rather hurtful, but I remember thinking, Who the heck is going to take him on?

Calvin remarried less than a year after our divorce. Our divorce was amicable. We pretty much divided everything in half. I was determined that there wouldn't be any acrimony, because of the children. I didn't expect him to remarry so soon, and I also didn't expect that he would marry such an idiot. She's twenty-seven years younger than he is. Now I'm convinced that he was seeing her when we were still together, because toward the end of our marriage, his cell phone rang, and he said, "I can't talk right now," and her number was on the phone. It turns out that her mother was a longtime patient of his who'd had a stroke years before, and Calvin took care of her. They have a baby now. Imagine—a baby at his age, and he didn't want to have children, let alone more children.

John moved in with me two months after Calvin was married. I felt torn about whether or not he should be living with us, but my kids were so supportive. They were very much in tune with me and wanted me to be happy. They didn't like their stepmother, although I kept telling them to give her a chance and be polite whether they liked her or not.

One thing that gnaws at me is that Calvin refused to wear a wedding ring when we were married; he said he was afraid he would lose it when he took it off to scrub. He wears one now, and he also goes to church on Sundays and takes Bible classes, and he's Jewish. Talk about a chameleon. However amicable a divorce is, it's those little things that end up getting to you. It was hard for me to deal with his new marriage and even harder when he had the new baby. It made me feel that everything I did to make our marriage work had been pointless and senseless because I was replaced so quickly. I think my kids felt the same way. They've asked, on occasion, why on earth he had another child when it seemed like he really never liked *them*—and I bite my lip because I don't want to say anything critical about him to the children.

John is wonderful to me. He's thoughtful and polite and adores me. He does all the dishes after we've had dinner. He stays with the kids and drives

them places. The kids really like him. The only impasse I hit was with my
two teenage daughters: John is not particularly good-looking, and Calvin is
quite dashing. John is short and slightly overweight and has graying hair,
and in the beginning, my daughters said that I could do better. But I explained to them that looks aren't everything. I told them how kind he is and
how well he loves me and how dearly I love him.

I look at my relationship with John as being as forever as anything can
be. I can picture myself growing old with him. And I would never cheat on
him. There's no need for that. I'm at a different stage in my life altogether,
and there would just be no point. Our sex life is absolutely wonderful. Often I wonder if it's him or my stage in life, but he's the best lover I've ever
had. The only thing is, John wants to get married, and I'm not sure how I
feel about that.

I was sad throughout the divorce despite the presence of John in my life.
I felt sad that I had not been appreciated. My overwhelming feeling was failure: failure to make my husband love me, failure to protect my children
from the stigma and future aggravations of divorce, failure to make this part
of my life successful. I guess we overachievers expect too much. Now I
know that I am strong and will continue to be strong for my children. You
find that you go through lots of stages in separation and divorce. Even after
the fact, I agonize over it sometimes. That's one of the reasons that I appreciate John so deeply. He is such a saint. He understands all this and he still
loves me.

Another thing that I am happy about is that I don't cry anymore.

Mrs. J

Mrs. J is a pretty, warm, vibrant forty-seven-year-old who lives with her husband and four children in a Connecticut suburb. A social worker by profession, she spends three afternoons a week counseling abused women. She wonders if what she suffers within her marriage is a form of abuse, although she would describe it more as neglect. She stays in her marriage for the children. She had an affair ten years ago, and although she dreams of one day being in the kind of relationship that will nourish her instead of starve her, right now she says she could never have an affair again. She is not one for frivolity, so she knows if she did, it would be because she had fallen in love again—and she can't bear the thought of sneaking around and loving another man when she can't be with him all the time.

I was thirty-seven years old and had just had a new baby, my fourth child. I had three boys, and this last-ditch effort resulted in a daughter. My whole life was perfectly planned. A baby every two years. Although my husband was content with three little boys, I wanted to try just one more time for the girl. And there she was. You would have thought that with three boys ages six, four, two, and a newborn, I would have been not only busy but content. True, there was a part of me that was extremely content, but days filled with baby talk and bottles and breast-feeding were arduous, to say the least. And then there was the housework.

It seemed that everyone in the suburbs had a housekeeper—most of the women had live-ins whether they worked or not—but I didn't. I quit my job in the city after I became pregnant with my second son, and as far as I was concerned, my new job was taking care of the kids and the house. So when the children napped or watched *Sesame Street*, I did a load of wash or cleaned one of the rooms. I didn't sit down for a moment, except to nurse. And I loved them more than I had ever loved anyone in my life. I loved the way they smelled, the way they curled against my flesh, the way they laughed and smiled and thought I was the center of the universe. But it dawned on me when my baby girl was six months old that my husband had not come near me in months. I teased him that maybe he was concerned if he so much as spit on me, I would conceive again, but he said that wasn't the case. Still, the once or twice we did connect, he used a condom like he was a stranger. He explained it by saying that he no longer trusted my diaphragm, even though it had worked every time, unless it was in the drawer when we were making love. As I said, I was organized. Babies were planned. But that condom became just one more thing to separate us.

There's no question that I was lonely. The flesh against flesh of my babies didn't substitute for the flesh of my husband. He was perpetually tired. He'd usually come home on the eight o'clock train—late enough so that the babies were sleeping and I'd gotten a second wind—but by the time he got to the house, it was after nine and he was exhausted. I'd managed to shower and change from the stale clothes I'd worn all day that reeked of milk and strained beans, and I looked pretty decent. I used to suggest that he might shower when he got home, to revive himself, but he said he wasn't interested in reviving himself—he just wanted to eat and get to sleep. Not to bed, mind you, to sleep.

Now, I looked pretty good. I never had a problem losing the baby weight, and I worked out as soon as the doctor gave me the go-ahead after each one was born. My husband and I would have dinner, and he'd read the paper while I did the dishes. I'd sort of try to cuddle up next to him, and sometimes we'd turn on the television. Invariably, he'd fall asleep on the couch, and I'd wake him around eleven and we'd get into bed—where there was nothing.

Around this time, I started to venture out a little bit more. The baby's feeding schedule was easier, and I wasn't quite as housebound. I pushed the double stroller through town with the two middle ones, held the oldest by the hand, and popped the baby into the Snugli. I felt like a mother duck. Usually, we went for these jaunts after school, since the oldest was in first grade and my second son was in half-day preschool. I took them to the toy store and the bookstore and the supermarket. Everywhere. Well, the man who owned the bookstore was someone I had known since I moved to town. He was warm and always spoke to the kids. And he was attractive: long dark hair tied in a ponytail and the most amazing steel-blue eyes. He reminded me of the guys I had dated in college. I was in the bookstore one day shortly before Christmas and asked for a certain book. He looked it up on the computer and said it was out of print, but he'd try to get a copy in time for Christmas, which was only three weeks away.

I was cleaning the house a few days before the holidays, preparing for the onslaught of relatives—my family and my husband's family—when the doorbell rang. I was in my cleaning clothes: black stretch pants, an oversize top, my hair on top of my head, and no makeup. The kids were on break from school, so the boys were playing in the basement, and the baby was napping. I opened the door with a can of Pledge in one hand and a rag in the other, figuring it was the postman with yet another package, but there was Dan from the bookstore. He handed me the book. I was so flustered that when I took it from him, I dropped the Pledge. He picked it up for me. I thanked him and felt my face get red. I realized that it was freezing outside and Dan was wearing only a sweater, and then it started to flurry. I motioned him to come inside, and we sat down in the living room. He was surprised that I did my own cleaning, and I told him how I felt that this was my job—the kids, the house, all that kind of stuff.

My oldest, Robbie, came up the stairs and recognized Dan, and Dan gave him a big hug and said, "Merry Christmas, buddy." Robbie's face just lit up. Then they arm-wrestled for a moment, and of course, Dan let Robbie win. It occurred to me that my husband never interacted physically with the boys at all. He was always saying stuff like he could hurt his back or his arm or his neck, and that was the last thing he needed. Then Robbie asked if he could have cookies, and I said that it was too close to dinner. Robbie said if I let him have cookies, he'd make a deal with me that he'd eat *all* his dinner. I told Robbie that I didn't make deals, but he could have *one* cookie. Robbie skipped off to get the cookie, and Dan said it was good that I didn't make deals with my kids. He said he disapproved of parents who bargained with their kids for either good behavior or obedience. Then Dan said that he always admired the way I handled the children and said I was a good mother. It made me feel so important and so satisfied.

We started talking. He told me that he had two sons and both were in college. He and his wife married very young and had the boys one after the other. He spoke sweetly about his wife. He was forthcoming and communicative in general, and I found myself drawn to him—not just physically and sexually but intellectually and, yes, emotionally. It made me realize how much I sorely missed conversation with my husband and with men altogether. My husband never was one for conversation. I would speak to him and feel that he wasn't listening and didn't hear half of what I said. Dan said it was funny that we had known each other for five years but had never really spoken. He remembered me with my second pregnancy, and he laughed and said that I appeared to *always* be pregnant. I told him that I had miscarried that second pregnancy at three months but got pregnant again a few months later. And I told him how that second pregnancy was the incentive for us to move here. Of course, right after we moved, I lost the baby. Dan looked stricken—a lot more stricken than my husband looked when I miscarried. My husband had said something like "It wasn't meant to be" and couldn't understand why I was grieving.

The baby woke up, and I went to get her, and Dan asked if I thought this was it now that I had my girl. I laughed and told him the kitchen was now closed, and he said that I looked great and appeared to be back in shape. Then the two middle boys came up from the basement with a LEGO they had made, and they dropped it and started to cry. I tried to help them and juggle the baby as I bent down, and then Dan took the baby from me. I helped them piece the LEGO back together, and they went back down to the basement. Dan said that he loved how patient I was with the boys. I didn't tell him, but I was thinking how sweet he was with the baby.

I nursed her discreetly while we talked, and it seemed so natural. We talked about Christmas and what our plans were and how winter was sort of gloomy. We talked about music that we both liked and books we liked, and after about an hour, he said he should get going. I walked him to the door, and he stopped and sort of hung his head and said that he didn't make a habit of making personal deliveries, but he really wanted to see me. I'd been in so many times that week for gifts, and he wanted to ask me something: Did I think we could have lunch sometime? My knee-jerk reaction was to tell him that I was married and it didn't feel right—but I didn't. Instead, I said that I didn't have a babysitter. He looked a little crestfallen, and then he apologized for being forward. I didn't want him to feel bad or to think I didn't want to see him again, so I said that after the holidays, when the two older boys were back in school, maybe I could manage something. Then he asked if he could kiss me. I remember nodding slowly. He kissed me very gently on the mouth and said he would call me. I was still holding the baby. My heart was pounding a mile a minute when he left. I felt hot and flushed—and guilty—but exhilarated and hopeful, because it was the first time in so long that a man had spoken to me, touched me, and made me feel like a woman, not just a wife and a mother.

The affair with Dan lasted for five years.

It's funny how it started. In the beginning, it wasn't sexual at all, although the tension was there, that's for sure. But I wasn't ready to be unfaithful to my husband. Dan held my hand and he kissed me, but that was all. I never did find a babysitter for the daytime, so I met him in the evenings. I'd meet him about once a week at this little bar that was part of a bed-and-breakfast about forty-five minutes away. I had a very good old girlfriend, Louise, who lived up that way and covered for me. I'd tell my husband that I was going to see her, and now that the baby was taking a bottle of breast milk at night, it was easier to get a sitter. My husband couldn't have cared less, because he was working. I always met Dan on the nights that Louise was out, and she'd tell her husband that she was meeting me and a bunch of the girls. Louise was telling the truth: She was meeting her girlfriends, but I wasn't part of the group. It worked perfectly. Anyway, Dan and I would sit and talk for hours. We'd have dinner and a little wine. And then I weaned my daughter from the breast altogether, because I wanted my life back.

The first time Dan made love to me was in the early summer. It was mid-June and we were on his sailboat. I called my sister and asked her to babysit for the day, something I'd never asked before. I didn't say where I was going. I just said I had errands to do, but I think she knew even then. She knows now. The baby was nearly a year old and knew her aunt well, so I didn't have to worry. I drove up to the beach and parked my car behind a restaurant and walked to the dock. At first I didn't see him, but then he stood up in his boat and waved. He was wearing a blue baseball cap, and he was sunburned and looked beautiful to me. I wore my bikini under my jeans. It's funny—I hadn't brought my diaphragm with me because I felt like that would have been so planned. I was still not convinced that I was having an affair with him, because we hadn't had sex yet. I'm telling you, I felt like I was sixteen again. There were no cell phones in those days. He had a ship-to-shore radio, and I had a beeper, but it never beeped (thank God). I was feeling guilty enough as it was, and if the beeper had gone off and something was wrong with one of the kids (the only reason my sister would have beeped me), I think I would have died right then and there—or wanted to.

We anchored the boat in a cove. It was during the week, so the lake was quiet. We went down to the cabin. There were two little beds on either side, and that's where it happened. I was so nervous. I hadn't been with anyone except for my husband in ten years. I stopped him sort of midway through and told him that I didn't have any birth control, but he said he'd had a vasectomy. I relaxed, and the strange thing was, I felt like I had been with him all my life.

I thought my sister could see right through me when I got home that evening, but she never said a word. She did ask me why I looked tanned, and I said that I had gone down to the beach and sat there for a few hours. She wagged her finger at me as she was leaving and told me that I'd better be careful. I said I didn't know what she meant, and she said, "Just think about what you're doing. You have four kids."

When my husband came home that night, I was worried that I would have a glow about me or not be able to look him in the eyes, but it wasn't like that at all. I gave him his dinner and made small talk and didn't care that the talk was small, because that day my talk had been profound with Dan, and topped off by lovemaking the way no one had made love to me in years. The only problem that evening was that I kept drifting off into thoughts about Dan. I wondered if I had made a fool of myself by being so easy, and whether Dan would call me again, and if I could ever go to his store again. I hardly slept that night. Dan called the next morning, and all my fears and apprehensions were quelled. I found some babysitters who would sit during the week, and I'd leave the kids for a few hours sometimes during the day. The bottom line is, where there's a will, there's a way. As time went on, I found I was more even-tempered and had fewer expectations of my husband. He didn't ask too many questions, and I was never gone for more than three hours at the most. I was always there to pick up the kids and always had dinner on the table.

But then the day came that Dan and I said we loved each other, and that was when things got very painful. I missed Dan like crazy when I wasn't with him. On the rare occasion when my husband wanted to have sex, I cringed. I felt like I was cheating on Dan, and that was so ironic, because when I was with Dan, I never felt like I was cheating on my husband. I remember one night we took a motel room for a few hours. I told my husband that I was out with the girls in the city. I implored him to be home early that night to relieve the babysitter so I could have a night out and he agreed. I remember that motel room so well—it was a place about a half hour away on the Hudson. That night Dan and I actually talked about the notion of divorcing our spouses and just being together. It was wrenching. When I went home, I felt so empty. My husband was sleeping and the kids were sleeping and I got into bed next to my husband and all I could think of was how could I possibly spend the rest of my life in this marriage when my heart belonged to someone else.

Needless to say, I was riddled with both guilt and grief. Guilt because I felt deceitful. Grief because I wondered whether I was killing my marriage and not giving it more of a chance. Grief because I wasn't with Dan and longed for him when we weren't together. On the weekends, my husband and I went out with friends and spent time with the kids and everything appeared to be fine. My husband was happy that I was with my girlfriends during the week and getting out of the house. It never occurred to him that I was having an affair, something that angered me sometimes, because it was another indication of how separate our lives were and how little he knew me or wanted to know me. For my husband, life went on—minimal conversation, rare times when we had sex (he didn't seem to notice that my body was there and my mind was elsewhere). It proved to me how superficial our marriage was. It made me weep.

Dan and I met at motels. We had sex in his van. We had sex in the warehouse of the bookstore, on his boat when the weather permitted, and one weekend we even managed to go away. I told my husband I was going to a spa in Massachusetts. I did go to the spa, but Dan took a room in a motel nearby, and although I had a facial, a massage, and two aerobics classes (just so they would appear on the bill), I was with Dan the entire time. It was rather risky, because it was just luck that neither of us ran into anyone we knew. He was a familiar figure in town, and we weren't *that* far from home.

The affair never ended with a breakup. It ended by attrition, when it got to the point where we both knew that it either had to stop or we had to be together. Well, neither of us wanted to break up our families. Neither of us had the courage to break up with each other, either. The times we were together became further apart, and the sex became less frequent, and one day we just realized that we were friends and that was how it had to be. We'd have lunch here and there, but it all got too sad. I still see him in town, but I go to a different bookstore now or order books online. Sometimes I look at him and can't believe we shared so much for so many years. I'm not in love with him anymore, and sometimes I wonder whether I've willed it to be that way or whether it wouldn't have lasted and I made the right decision not to run off with him.

The one thing I do know is that I will never, could never, have that kind of love affair again, because as glorious as it was, it hurt so deeply. It took too much energy to sneak around. I was always afraid of being caught in a lie or being caught altogether. As for my marriage, the more things change, the more things stay the same, and our future (at least in my mind) remains uncertain. The kids are growing up (the "baby" is in fifth grade now), and

I've gone back to work. I'm a social worker at a local shelter for abused women. I know this sounds like a terrible thing to say, but sometimes I find myself almost envying the women who come in with blackened eyes and swollen lips, because *their* wounds are visible. We can look at them and reach out to them and want to protect them. We see and hear and feel their justification when they say they want to escape their marriages and begin new lives. The wounds I suffer are invisible. They are wounds to my soul. My husband's attitude toward me, his benign neglect, undermines my self-esteem. When I am around my husband, I feel worthless and undesirable. If I tell people how he makes me feel, even my friends, they assume I am either a lonely housewife, or the dynamic in our marriage is off. I guess what I'm trying to say is that sometimes I wish I had a visible bruise to show someone where I could be saying, "Look, look what he did to me."

My husband and I spend the weekends watching the kids playing sports, and his hours at work are even longer than they were. Our sex life is still lousy. We don't talk to each other. If I broach the subject of our marriage, my husband's fatigue becomes more pronounced, and he asks me angrily what it is that I want from him, since he works "like a slave," and that's the end of the discussion. But to look at us from the outside, people think we're just the perfect pair.

I heard from a mutual friend that Dan is having an affair with another woman in town. Why did the friend tell me? To protect me, I think. I'd been thinking about Dan lately, and although I know he's not the answer for me, I get lonely. Dan's new lady is in her thirties, the way I was, and I wonder if that's Dan's targeted age group and if he tells her that he loves her the way he told me. I wonder if he's with her because she makes him feel younger or reminds him of me. There is a cynic in me who wasn't there ten years ago. It makes me wonder how naive I was ten years ago and if that same gossip circle was talking about me and Dan. I run into Dan from time to time, and he talks to me about his wife and kids in the way he did before I "knew" him.

He exudes an attitude of absolute purity when it comes to his family. Sometimes it makes me sad, because no one knows that we really loved each other. Maybe people suspected that we had an affair, since there's talk about this woman and Dan now, but I doubt anyone ever knew the depth of our relationship. I wonder if this woman goes on his sailboat the way I used to. I refuse to believe that he's in love with her.

I can't help but wonder if this is all there is. If life with Dan would have been different or gradually become empty, like what I have now. Looking back, I don't think Dan was ever prepared to leave his wife. Men don't leave. And I couldn't have left, either. Maybe I didn't love Dan enough. More important, it was about the children and our family, and it would have been too great a sacrifice. But one day, someday, I want to be with a man who loves me and lets me love him the way I loved Dan, this time for real. The sad thing is that after all this, I still want that with my husband. That feels like the greatest and most unrequited fantasy of them all.

MRS. K

Mrs. K is a passionate, brilliant seventy-year-old who lives out west and who doesn't look a day over fifty-five. She has great insight not only into herself but into those around her. Her fifty-year marriage is platonic and has been for the last twenty-five years. She is comfortable and peaceful. When she was in her forties and fifties, her life was edgy and at times even tumultuous. She had a half-dozen or so affairs. She wishes her marriage were different. She still craves passion, but she questions how life would be, whether it would be better, if she were alone. She is resigned and philosophical, believing that we don't get everything we want.

My husband was my college sweetheart—but not my first college sweetheart. I knew him casually, and we went out for the first time in May, and I slept with him in October. I became pregnant the first time we slept together, so we got married. We were so young. We stayed in school and graduated, but by the time I was twenty-six, I had three kids. There was no question in my mind back then about fidelity and monogamy: It was just there and that was it. That changed when I got older.

We had a tough marriage. Looking back, I believe that our marriage was troubled because we just never grew up. He was involved in a horrible family business, and I was much more ambitious in many ways than he is or was. I started doing a little bit of traveling because I was on a lot of committees and boards, and I think that is always a telling time to learn about yourself— you're away from home and on your own, and then you have the feeling that you're a person again, not the mother of three kids and someone's wife.

A darkness manifested itself in this personal life that I lived. Part of it is that I feel my sexuality has always been problematic. Somewhere I have the autobiography I wrote when I was a sophomore in college. In it I talked about the closeness of my family, which was, in many ways, claustrophobic. The autobiography spoke about the need to break away from that claustro- phobia and the intense desire that I had to individuate at an early age. When I was young, and perhaps even more so as I got older, I always had a public life and a personal, secret life. Maybe everyone feels that way—I don't really know.

When the kids were young, my husband worked all the time, and under that protective umbrella of work, he didn't have to deal with anything. For certain, he missed our children's childhoods, and I know he wasn't the only man of his generation like that, but still. I know a woman my age who had two daughters, and yet her husband was the one who always got up at night with the children when they awakened. He was the fairy-tale wonderful fa- ther and loving husband. Now he has terrible Parkinson's. My friend refuses to institutionalize him. They have twenty-four-hour-a-day help at home, but it is really my friend who cares for him. Their daughters are both accom- plished; one is a psychiatrist, and she felt her mother's behavior was over the top, but my friend explained that because he was always so kind and loving, she couldn't bear to put him anywhere she wasn't certain he would be cared for perfectly. I just saw him and he's totally unresponsive. These are life's ironies.

We had some house guests once at our little weekend home in Marin County, a married couple we'd met through mutual friends. I was forty and enamored of them. They were bright, elegant, lovely, warm people. They were joggers, and I started jogging with them—mostly because I wanted to be around them, since I found them so stimulating and fantastic. The woman lived a much more urbane life than I ever had, and she told me about someone we both knew who'd had an affair. I remember saying to her that I couldn't even imagine what that would be like.

Shortly after that weekend, I went off to a conference and drove two hours to get there with a colleague of mine, a man who was slightly younger than I and divorced. During the drive, he told me that he was very attracted to me. I was in shock because I didn't see myself in any way as attractive. It was the *last* thing I could imagine anyone noticing about me. I felt that people didn't notice me in physical ways, though I knew they noticed me because I was smart and hardworking and I got a lot of attention in those areas, but the physical wasn't something that ever occurred to me. When we got back after that conference, he and I had a brief affair. We slept together once— that was all. It was radical and revolutionary behavior for me. I couldn't quite figure out what I was doing or why I was doing it, but I did know that my marriage was in very bad shape, and I knew that my self-image was minus zero. That was all on the personal, private level—in the outside world, I was doing just fine.

I think the problem with my marriage was that I had dreams and ideas and physical needs that my husband wasn't meeting. I would say that our marriage was in serious trouble and I would tell him that we had to get real help in order for us to survive, and my husband's response was that I was frigid. Again, I suggested we needed help and that I was happier when we were apart, and he said that was because I was selfish. If there's one thing I'm not, it's selfish. I am many things, but I am not selfish. It was so pointless, so I filed for divorce, but I filed for a no-fault divorce because I thought, No one's at fault—it's just the fault of our youth and immaturity and the pressures of family life.

I was living in San Francisco and doing good work at Stanford, and my husband was staying mostly at our weekend house. I think he was living with someone there. I'll never know for sure, because I never went there during that period of time. Around then, my first college sweetheart reappeared. He and his wife had just relocated to San Francisco. They had a bunch of kids. We had an affair. It was very touching and poignant. His marriage was a mess, and he needed a lot of help.

When we ended, I met another man who was the most unlikely match for me. I met him through friends at a dinner party. He was ten years older than I and had a very troubled California-style life: He'd been married a few times (once to a movie star—that whole crazy thing) and had made and lost millions of dollars. His life was a shambles. The only thing he had left was a membership at a fancy golf club, because a long time ago, he'd bought himself a lifetime membership. So he was reduced to poverty, but he could play golf with his buddies, which I found rather amusing. He was the most incredible lover imaginable. He was exquisite in bed and such a nice person, but he was nuts. Truly, we had little in common.

Then I had to have a hysterectomy. I couldn't even get out of bed after the surgery. I was weak and deeply anemic because I'd lost so much blood along the way. My husband, of course, knew about my surgery, but I wouldn't see him. I didn't want him near me. I wanted to be something and someone more than I was when I was with him. I wanted to be freer and happier, and with him around me, that was impossible. It was tough on my kids when I was sick. They'd never seen me sick a day in my life, and though they were young adults, they were still shaken. Finally, I relented and let my husband move back in with me—I suppose because I was in such a weakened state and wanted my kids to be comforted knowing that I wasn't alone. And my husband wanted to come back. I guess I was too worn out to argue. Besides, he was traveling a lot, so I figured it would be fine.

There were other men after that, and I would ask them all the same question: Do you think I'm frigid? And they would all roar with laughter and think I was joking. But the serious affairs were with the people I'd known when I was younger. I felt that in some ways, I was going through that late-adolescent period that I had missed. I don't wear a wedding band. I never put it back on. I've been living with my husband, but we haven't slept together in twenty-five years—not since he moved back in. I can hardly believe it myself. He's such a limited person, however, that we've never spoken about it. What does he do for sex? I have no idea. We really live as roommates. We have two rooms, although sometimes we share a room. We've been together for so long, and the comfort of having a person in your life is not casual when you're older. As a marriage goes, given our passionate beginning, I look at him sleeping in the other room, and sometimes the whole thing feels so unreal. I look at us now, and I look back, and I wonder how we ended up this way.

It's not all simple. It's not that my husband and I married too young or that he's limited and I'm ambitious or that we had a troublesome child. There are many subtopics within my marriage. I had parents who were deeply in love and committed to each other, and that was the vision that I had for my life, but I never met anyone who was the perfect person for *me*. I think I understood my relationships with the two men from my past, from high school and college. In later years, when we were having the affair, I asked my old college boyfriend what he thought of the relationship we had, and he said that when he came back to college to find me after we broke up, he heard that I was married. He also said that if he and I had gotten married, the marriage would have lasted only three or four months because I was a tiger. I was shocked. I always think of myself as mild, and he's a strong, nice, masculine, athletic guy. It fascinated me that he perceived me that way. The truth is that he felt I was too strong a personality for him. He never would have been able to tame me, to domesticate me. I mean, he has a ton of kids now, and they were all his idea—that was what he wanted in a wife. He had a very bright older brother who was a college professor, and I often thought that I met the wrong brother—the older brother was complex and literary and challenging—but anyway, that was that.

The high school boyfriend, the one who ended up teaching at Stanford, was a man I cared for very deeply. When we met again and had our affair, he wanted me to meet his wife and become part of his life. I said, "Forget that—that's not for me." They eventually got divorced and he married a colleague and I've heard through mutual friends that they're still living happily ever after. I was disappointed when I heard that he remarried, but I also knew that he and I would never change our lives for each other, since after they married, he relocated to the Northeast. He told me about his new wife—he kept saying that she was just so sweet. Well, I'm not sweet. I think he got what he was looking for in life, though, so I'm happy for him. I spoke to him frequently after he remarried. We'd talk about the books we've read and things of that nature, but when his new wife found out we were still in touch, she didn't like it. She was right not to like it, because he and I still had a strong connection.

I think I am tied to my husband, though. I think I was tied to him as soon as we had the kids. He finally became a decent father, and he loves being a grandparent. He's become a warmer, sweeter person, but unfortunately, the physical part is just gone from our marriage and gone from him. Before I was sixty, I gave myself a gift of three years of very excellent therapy with a wonderful therapist, and I think I pretty much know now why things are what they are. The therapist campaigned for me to leave my husband and live my own life, but I am resigned to the fact that you just don't get everything in life. I have a dear cousin who had a wonderful marriage until her husband died about ten years ago. Before she had that wonderful marriage, she had been engaged to another man with whom she was deeply in love, and her family disapproved. She had an affair of the heart with that other man all throughout her marriage. That man has also died. Now she's gone on to find yet another extraordinary love affair and believes, philosophically, that you can have it all. But I don't believe that.

Looking back, I don't think even my parents had it all, at least not in conventional ways. When my younger sister died in her forties, it wiped out any semblance of wholeness in the family. My mother lived for fifteen years after my sister died. My father lived about six years. He had a temper, but he was such a sweet man. I'm a lot like him, so I understand him. He could control his emotions unless you put him up against a wall, and then forget it. As I said, I'm a lot like him. So when my mother wanted to do things that no one else in the world wanted to do, my father smiled. He might have gotten a little upset to begin with, but he also knew that she needed to do the unlikely and needed a lot of freedom, and I think he liked that about her. If he didn't at times, well, she filled his life with many things he wanted and needed, and that was enough for him.

Sometimes I think that had I been in a better marriage, my life would have been even more of a struggle. Maybe I wouldn't have been as compelled to accomplish as much in my life as I've accomplished had my marriage been less fraught with difficulty and had my husband been more ambitious. I think that for a woman of my generation, I was more fortunate than others. I never felt I had to compete with my husband, because it took him a very long time to figure out who he was and what he wanted to be. I was very happy when he and I were separated for a year. One could think that the hysterectomy put me in a weakened position and made me take him back—that he was a safe haven for me—but it's quite the contrary: *He* was the one who was truly lost during that time. I was the safe haven for *him*.

Sometimes my husband will mention the fact that we have no romance, but he always mentions it in an offhand way. To really get to the bottom of it, we'd have to talk about what happened, and I don't think he wants to—and I'm not willing to lie to make him feel better. It's a strange time in my life, because many of my friends' husbands have died, and in this small group we have, three spouses have died out of five couples. I'm grateful for what there is. When I am productive, and I remain productive, then I am happy. We have loads of friends. I still feel a sense of freedom when my husband and I are away from each other for a week here and there, but I don't kid myself: Life wouldn't be better if I were alone. As I said before, I am older now. Being older is lonely by itself. At least my husband is here. At least we're friends. I'm sad that we're not lovers as well, but as I keep telling myself, I guess we just can't have everything.

MRS. L

Mrs. L is in her early fifties and divorced. She lives in a suburb of Detroit with her three teenage sons. She works full-time, has many friends, is involved with the school and the community, and once upon a time was in a marriage that was not merely unsatisfying but rather horrifying. No one knew but her. Although she doesn't know what the future holds, she remains optimistic and is fiercely independent.

I adored my ex-husband, Max. Possibly for the wrong reasons, but I adored him. He was this handsome, charming, successful, powerful man who was wild about me and made me feel like the most beautiful, smart, funny woman alive.

I met Max when he was my client. I didn't know how old he was until we had dated two or three times. The funny thing is, I thought he was younger than he was, and he thought I was older, so we were both surprised. I was twenty-six and he was forty. I was never married, and he'd been married once before. It was strange, because he would talk about his son who was in college, and I would talk about college since I'd just graduated a few years before. Looking back, I was more sophisticated in many ways than Max was. I was also very needy.

I went to bed with him relatively quickly, on our third date, to be exact.

And shortly after that, he took me to the Kentucky Derby for the weekend. And then he took me to the Oscars, the Tonys, the Emmys, Wimbledon . . . everywhere. It was unbelievable. It was very heady stuff. We dated for four months, he proposed, we moved in together, and a year and a half later, we were married.

Our sex life was never great. It was a reasonably active sex life, but he wasn't terribly creative or enthusiastic—it was more a show of affection. But it didn't matter too much to me at the time, because I'd had so much sex before that, and it felt good to settle into a nice, comfortable married-type sex life—or so I thought. He told me that he hadn't slept with his first wife for the last three years of their marriage. He said he simply wasn't attracted to her. He also admitted that he was angry, and that their marriage was filled with anger. Foreshadowing, I guess, because years later, those were all the reasons he gave me when our marriage failed. He was not unfaithful to his first wife; he just masturbated a lot. During our engagement, when I told my therapist all those things, she said, "Get out. Please don't marry him." But I thought I was going to fix it. I was determined.

When we were living together, we didn't have sex frequently, but we had sex regularly for about eight months. And then one day we went to visit his parents for a week, and I asked him if we could have sex when we were there. "What? You can't go a week without sex?" he asked.

I said no. Well, that was the kiss of death: Once I had introduced the concept of need, my need, into our relationship—like the notion that I needed to have sex once a week (at least) with him—his head went right to obligation, and that was the end. We didn't have sex on our honeymoon. It was real performance anxiety, but it was so humiliating that I'd move my diaphragm from place to place around the room so that the hotel housekeeper wouldn't know we weren't having sex. And there we were on the Italian Riviera—it could have been romantic and sexy. I didn't say anything to him that early on, but after a while, I did. Did I want to get out of the marriage then? No, I still wanted to fix him. I thought I could fix him and everything else about us, about him. I was still in love with him. Not to mention that I wasn't about to be defeated. You know, it was like this: "Look, world (also known as 'Look, Mom')—see what I got? He's handsome, charming, powerful, rich, and he adores me—therefore, I must have worth." It was irrelevant that when we got into bed and closed the bedroom door, he hid behind a stack of newspapers and magazines and ignored me. The world saw a different picture.

From the minute he met me, he knew that I wanted children. He knew how important it was for me to have children because I told him. After about three years of marriage, when I said I was ready to have kids, he'd changed his mind. And he said it so dispassionately. I told him that I wasn't talking about buying a dog—I was talking about *having children*. His excuse was that he didn't know if our marriage was strong enough.

Our sex life was lousy: We'd gone from once a week to once a month to once every few months, so it wasn't like I could get pregnant by accident. He kept saying that he wanted to wait and see if the marriage got better, and the translation was that he wanted to see how well I could behave myself—if I could take care of all his needs and demand nothing, and if so, he would make me a baby.

We were childless and married ten years when I had an affair. It was with my boss, Charlie, who was the quintessential stud, my age, married with children. And he was built like a brick shithouse, gorgeous, and loved women, which my husband did *not*. Charlie made me feel beautiful and desirable and sexy. One afternoon we had a presentation, and afterward we took his Porsche out to the beach—he said it would be nice to walk along the sand and talk about our meeting. Unquestionably, I was attracted to him, though I truly wasn't planning to do anything. But he made me feel not only sexy but sexually attractive, something that my husband hadn't made me feel for a long time. When my husband had to buy me a present, he'd give me something like a frilly peasant shirt—not even remotely my style; he wanted me to be his little girl and dress the part. Anyway—and forgive me, I tend to digress when I think back on my marriage; I remember things that practically screamed at me but I didn't hear—my boss and I walked and talked, and when we got back to the parking lot, I leaned against the car and looked out over the water and said how beautiful it was, and suddenly, he kissed me. And kissed me again. We kept kissing, and it felt so great.

My husband and I had bought a weekend house, and I started to go out there on Thursday evenings after work, and Charlie would meet me there. Charlie and I became lovers. Max and I had a pool table, and Charlie would just put me on that pool table and make love to me. He had studied at one point to be an opera singer, and he would be in the shower with me on his knees, doing what he was doing to me and singing an aria. He wrote me songs and poetry. Was he in love with me? Was I in love with him? No. We lasted about a year and a half. Sure, I was infatuated, and when I had to be at home with my husband for the weekend, my head was someplace else and I couldn't wait to get back to work.

I met Charlie's wife at one point. She was sweet and very dumb. She was the female counterpart, sexually, of my husband. My therapist believed that my husband looked the other way—that he knew I was having an affair. I think that's true. At one point Max found a love poem that Charlie had written to me, about a married man falling in love with a married woman. He handed it to me. Can you imagine? I was beet red and twitching, but Max didn't ask a thing. I mean, Charlie and I would be at business dinners and functions together with our spouses, and people I knew would take me aside and tell me that the chemistry between us, the energy, was palpable. If Max noticed, he didn't let on. My therapist also suggested that Max was grateful for Charlie—after all, Charlie was doing what Max didn't want to have to do. Personally, I think my husband was just oblivious.

On some level, I knew that Charlie and I weren't truly in love, even though we said "I love you." I think even in those younger years—or maybe they're colored now, as I look back—I knew this wasn't true love. It was a game, but it was okay. I never had any intention of leaving my husband for Charlie. I thought about leaving my husband, but not for Charlie.

And then I got pregnant and didn't know whether or not it was my husband's or Charlie's, since Max and I had sex before I became pregnant. Charlie and I were so spontaneous that although he'd use a condom, sometimes he didn't. It was more that we were caught up in the heat of passion, and it felt so much better without the condom. My diaphragm was too inconvenient.

I went for the sonogram, and they said the baby wasn't growing, even though there was a heartbeat. They told me that I would undoubtedly miscarry in the next few days—a week at the most—so there I was, walking around pregnant for the first time, dying to have a baby and knowing I was going to lose it. My husband couldn't have cared less. For him, it was an easy out.

So one evening after Max and I had dinner, I went into "labor," for lack of a better term. It was predicted. I called to Max, but he was on a business call, so I went into the bathroom and took a pot from the kitchen, and as the fetus poured out of me, I scooped it into the pot. Max went to sleep. I called a taxi service and then called my doctor, and he met me at the ER, where he did a D & C without anesthesia. I was so beat up. I was such a mess. I lied to the doctor and said that Max was out of town. Then I took a taxi back home and got into bed.

My husband left for work the next morning before I awakened, and when he came home around seven the next night, I was in bed. He hadn't called me all day. Well, he came into the bedroom and stood at the foot of the bed and said that he didn't think he could go through this again. I asked him, "What are you saying? Are you saying you don't want to try and have another child?" He said that wasn't it, but he wouldn't answer me. He just stood there and stared at me. I rolled over and went to sleep.

So, why did I stay with him? Because I wanted children. What if I didn't find someone in time for my biological clock? I became pregnant again about a year later and still didn't know whether it was my husband's or Charlie's, but I broke it off with Charlie. I was so afraid of losing the next baby that I decided I wasn't going to have wild sex anymore. It was better just being with my husband and having no sex. During the pregnancy, Max wouldn't even sleep in the same room as me. He wanted nothing to do with me at all.

Our marriage was horrendous the first year after I had the baby. My first son was born, and they put him into my husband's arms, and he walked away and turned his back on me and stood in a corner of the room holding the baby and singing to him. He made it quite clear that he loved him and I was nothing. We had no sex for a long, long time after that. I was in a depression and felt so overwhelmed and lonely. I started working again—not for Charlie—but working and having an infant was hard and stressful. I felt like I had so much on my plate. I'd ask Max to help me. I was tired. I wasn't sleeping. I wanted him to be supportive emotionally, physically, and he turned to me and said, "Puerto Ricans do this with ten children." Nice, huh?

I wanted to matter to him. Forget the notion that he might even consider making love to me. I just wanted him to touch me, desire me, appreciate me, anything. There was nothing.

We went for marriage counseling and sex therapy. One session, the therapist told Max to leave the room because she wanted to talk to me alone. She couldn't understand why I stayed with him. We didn't see her after that session. We went to another therapist who asked Max why he hadn't slept with me in so long. We left him as well, since Max had no answer and felt like he was being attacked. Then we went to someone else who suggested we just sit in bed and talk or play backgammon or something and start touching. Max wouldn't have any part of that, either. I would have done anything. I wanted my marriage to work. In spite of everything, I still loved him.

Now that we're divorced, I see that Max doesn't like women. He's uncomfortable and afraid of them and incapable of feeling desire, and it's so sad. When we were married, I would tell him that I adored him, but he made me feel so undesirable that I would weep. One time he was brutally honest: "The more you ask for something, the less I want to give it to you." It wasn't a statement born out of anger. It appeared to be more of a confession. It slowly became clear to me that work was his orgasm, and I asked him, and he said that was about right. Then he told me not to try anything funny, like wearing something sexy to bed, because he didn't want to be put in the position where he viewed me as an obligation. I went to see yet another therapist, thinking maybe Max was impotent and didn't want to tell me. The therapist said that impotent men are saying, "Honey, I can't," and my husband was saying, "I won't." I knew the therapist was correct, although it was painful to hear. I knew for a fact that Max had erections, but he'd go into the bathroom and masturbate instead of coming to me. There it was, right in my face: "See, I *can,* but I *won't.* Not with you."

Despite all the therapists who told me to leave him, I ignored the advice because I wanted more children and I was still determined to make the marriage work. I told Max that I wanted another baby because I didn't want our son to be an only child. He said we would have another baby only if he was another boy, so we went to a fertility expert who takes the sperm and spins it and supposedly separates the chromosomes. This worked really well for Max, because then I was artificially inseminated and he didn't have to come near me. All he had to do was go into the bathroom at the doctor's office and masturbate and then give the sperm to the doctor. We did that three times. He sat in the waiting room while I was in the examination room with my legs up in the air waiting for the sperm to take. It took one try and I became pregnant with twin boys. I was certain that would heal whatever ailed Max. I have to say, he was thrilled.

The boys were four months old when Max and I had sex for the first time in years, and I got pregnant. Max said I had to have an abortion, and I did. I went alone. It never occurred to me to keep the baby and leave my husband. I had three little boys at home. When I got home, my friend Sheila was there. She'd stayed with the kids and I got into bed. I was bleeding and sore and weary. When Max came home, I asked him to go to the drugstore for me, since I needed some supplies. I asked him to please take the kids, which he did. I watched him walking out the door with the children, and I remember loving and hating him.

I still can't think about that abortion. It was a girl.

I was so unhappy, but I kept wondering whether our problems stemmed from Max or me. I'd ask my mother and she'd say, "He's a good father and a good provider. So what if you don't have sex? Go sleep with someone else." I remember one time when I was breast-feeding the twins, and Max stood in front of me and said, "I hate you. I just hate you." I started to cry. I guessed he hated me because I was tired and anxious and demanding. How could it not be that?

I still stayed with him. Looking back now, I realize how cruel he was.

There were a few catalysts that made me leave him. After the twins were born, he would take the three kids into a room and shut the door and leave me out. It made me nuts. We were fighting all the time and went back into counseling. Again, the therapist asked him why he wasn't sleeping with me, and he said he was angry at me. The therapist asked if he ever felt loving toward me. He didn't answer. We were falling apart. We were both angry, and I was needy. Was his anger directed at me? I guess some of it was. I knew he hated women, hated his mother—and hated me. I represented all the things he didn't want. What he fell in love with was an independent, attractive young woman, and he ended up with a mother who needed help with the children.

One day I had the kids in the backyard, and Max was doing paperwork in the house. The kids were just being so cute. My oldest son was pushing the twins on two swings, one after the other, and I called to Max to come look for a moment. The kids were just so precious. Max came out of his office and started screaming at me. At the top of his lungs. I looked at him and said I couldn't do this anymore.

What I didn't know was that he was having an affair. I found out shortly after that. I found receipts for a hotel room on top of his dresser. I took them and copied them and got myself a lawyer. I never confronted him. Then a friend of mine saw him and his lover at a restaurant and called to tell me. It was actually our anniversary. I still didn't tell him that I knew.

When I finally confronted him about the affair (and he's still with her), he denied it. He still denies that he was having the affair that last year of our marriage. He found an apartment in the city and moved out.

I just wanted to be alone with my children. I wanted to be a good mother. I didn't love Max anymore. The first weekend he had the kids for an overnight, I went to a group of divorced women who all had children, and I met some nice women and made a couple of good friends.

If I ever remarry again—and it's been a dozen years since we separated— I would never marry someone who had Max's problem, which, as I see it, was a problem with desire. One of the myriad sex therapists we went to asked me, "What if he was injured and he couldn't have sex? Then what?" I said it wouldn't matter because we could still hug and kiss. I've been saying "sex," but it wasn't about sex so much as it was about *desire*. Max had no desire for me, and I needed to be desired. I'm in my fifties now. I would never, ever marry a man who didn't desire me. Add to that part that I am now menopausal and my desire is waning. Back in the days with Max, my desire and my libido were at a peak. I guess I missed the boat.

When I was in my late forties, I met the guy I'm seeing now—Rob. He recently went through a messy divorce, but he loves women. He loves every smell and every touch, and he does desire me, but I won't marry him. In some ways, I think he's still a child. There's no question about it that I gravitate to the wrong type of men. A friend of mine pointed out to me (she happens to be a therapist) that it's very empowering to give and to take care of someone. I definitely gave a lot, and I don't receive as well as I give. I mean, Rob has to tell me twelve times a minute when we're having sex that I can just lie there and let him give to me—and I feel guilty instead of accepting that it gives him pleasure. My mother used to tell me to "always be a giver, don't be a taker," so I learned well. I think she believes that I'm not fundamentally lovable— and that she's not, either—and this is the legacy she passed on to me.

How do I feel about women who cheat on their husbands? I think that sex is private. It's none of my business. I am the last person to judge. But there are risks. I wouldn't feel good about someone who wasn't smart or aware of what he was doing. I don't like home wreckers. But it takes two to tango. For me, it's not a moral issue. My friends knew about my affair—some because I told them and others because they guessed. I never felt judged by them. Even my mother knew. I never flaunted it, though. I didn't want to get caught.

My current therapist asked me why I didn't demand that Max be with me the day that I was miscarrying or the day that I had the abortion. She asked me why I didn't just tell him that I needed him to be there for me. Well, I didn't feel entitled. I was raised by a sadistic father and a narcissistic mother, and it never occurred to me to ask for something. Friends asked why I didn't call them, either. That's just not me, and to a large degree, it still isn't. It's something that never would have occurred to me.

I will never again lock myself into a relationship that doesn't enhance my life. The best thing is, now I have girlfriends who enhance my life.

MRS. M

Mrs. M is forty-one years old, divorced, and living in Vermont. She was married for thirteen years and has two children. She is happy in her life. Her children are well adjusted and happy, her job is rewarding, her friendships are true, and the man in her life is loving and honest. She spends each day trying to make her life even better. She tries to unravel the past and look to the future and live in the present. She is determined to find love but knows where the traps lie and steps over them adeptly. Once too filled with expectation, she now approaches life and love more realistically—although she still has irrepressible romance in her soul.

B ecause I failed so miserably the first time I ever loved someone, as a teenager, everything about love was difficult for me as I grew older. There was a stretch of time, about two years, when I believed love was something that could be held on to for a moment at a time and that it was reckless and false to try to do anything else beyond enjoy its presence and be ready to wave goodbye at the drop of a hat. So I was promiscuous, but it didn't take long before I found it hard to get up and leave.

After college, I joined the military. I met my husband in Germany. We dated for about a year, and he asked me to marry him. I likely would have said no, except there was no other way for us to remain in the same place, due to financial realities. I felt that my husband—my then-boyfriend—was gentle, simple, grounded, and steady, and I was the complete opposite. He was very quiet. I couldn't stop talking. I told him frankly that I didn't think I was ready for marriage, but I would try. The only argument we ever had while courting was over a remark I made about his mother.

I was somewhat tempted by someone other than my husband within the first year of our marriage. There was really nothing but a little kissing—this third party was in love with someone else, and we were basically friends. I think I was just rebelling against the idea of marriage. It didn't take me long to become devoted to trying to be a good wife by standard measures. Surprisingly, it wasn't that hard, though I was aware all along that we weren't growing together.

I remained faithful for about nine years. There was a little bit of flirting and kissing with a couple of people while I was finishing college in the States and my husband was still in Germany, but otherwise, I didn't think about finding a relationship outside of my marriage for a very long time. I wished that my husband and I could be in love, but I knew we weren't. It wasn't exactly painful, for a few reasons. We had children, and that kept me busy, and my husband left that whole world to me. I loved being a mother to the extreme. Having the kids was the beginning of my healing from the bottom up.

Another reason I didn't find it hard to remain faithful was because I felt old. There was even a period of time, when my first child was about two—about four years into my marriage—that I felt completely dead: hopeless about my marriage. I felt around ninety years old. I went to stay with my mom. There was nothing in particular that brought this on. My husband did go out a lot with his friends. We had little money. I had almost no support network (we chose our home to be close to his family). These were all contributing factors, but I think what got to me is that my husband and I had come to a place where we had almost no verbal communication. It seemed as if he literally couldn't hear when I spoke to him. It was scary. I began to fear him because of the huge distance between us. I couldn't picture us anymore—not in the present or the future.

I don't remember how long I stayed at my mother's, but he came and got me, and I guess we had some sort of reconciliation. He became more accessible and attentive, I suppose. I felt better and allowed myself to feel for him again. I was hoping for some positive changes, and within a year, I became pregnant again. I worked hard to help my husband find what he wanted to do with his life. I told him how important it was to be passionate about his work. He went back to school, and at least on the surface, things began to get a little better. He seemed to think that most of our problems were related to money, but I didn't agree. I did all of the substantial talking for us, I was the one to communicate. I went to marriage counseling alone for a few months. I came home and told my husband things the therapist had told me. I changed my hairstyle. I thought about wearing sexy lingerie, although that wasn't me. I tried to be more organized and punctual. It was at about the midpoint in our marriage when I realized the bottom line was that I hadn't done all the things I could do to make things better between us, and I wasn't going to leave or give up until I did. I was able to let go of a ton of bitterness and think mostly in terms of what I could do, not what he needed to do, to improve things. We tried to go on dates with each other, mostly to the movies. He wasn't an explorer in any sense of the word, and he didn't initiate anything. Everything we did together was at my suggestion. I thought several times, and did say to him, that it didn't matter where we went or what we did if we could only find a way to let each other know that we were happy together. I wanted us to be joyful. My husband thought that my giddy childlike side was pretty silly. He didn't exactly put me down, and we never argued about anything, but he couldn't join me in any substantial way. And I couldn't be free with him.

The big turning point for me was when I found a way to start writing again. This came about because I was in so much pain and began to find it more and more difficult to mother my children. My whole life was about running from one thing to another and constantly trying to please everyone and feeling, at the same time, like a failure. Writing was the only thing I have ever felt passionate about doing, and it didn't take me too long before I began to really look at what had happened with my first love. Going back there caused me to literally gasp for air. But somehow I found a way to keep breathing and look around me, and I knew that I was healing.

After another agonizing year, I felt twenty years younger. My body looked different to me, and it felt different. I wanted more than ever to be in love. These were thoughts that came to me unformed, not planned, and nearly subconsciously.

I began to have an affair with a man who was related to my mother's lover. He lived eight hundred miles away from me. It was like being in a different world when I went to see him. I felt safe with him because I'd known him at least superficially for years and trusted his brother, my mother's lover, a great deal. I didn't initiate the affair, but when he suggested that we get together, I said yes quite eagerly and let myself fall in love almost without a second thought. It saved my life to feel this much for the first time since I was a teenager. There was almost no thought in my head except that I wanted this person's love and I wanted to give love. It was all made possible logistically because my mother was sick and I was helping out with her work. I did have to go home a few months later. Before I returned, I told my husband about the affair, and he came to get me and the kids. We attempted to work things out, but that never got done. There was some waffling on my part. I told my husband that the affair wasn't completely over. He barely forgave me. I felt lucky, though, because I had a legitimate way out of the affair. I realized the person I was involved with was self-destructive to an extent I couldn't handle. He drank to excess, for one thing. I was worried for my children. My husband was like a rock. He meant family to me. He may have been emotionally unavailable, but he was solid.

I began to work on writing projects more than ever and became happier. We had more fun as a family and bought our first house—next door to someone I fell in love with a year later. Before falling in love again, I felt that maybe love was not in my stars. I thought that maybe I should just be content with what I had. That maybe when my husband was an old man, he would finally be able to show me that he loved me.

So, this neighbor of mine was wonderful. He had a similar quality to my first boyfriend in that he was larger than life, unashamed, took risks like crazy, made a stand, was passionate about everything he liked. He was everything I had ever dreamed of, and oddly, I didn't feel a strong physical attraction to him at first. The physical part came slowly.

He helped me sort through my marriage. He gave me talking room to begin to mention the possibility of ending my marriage. I had never felt assertive about saying that I really *had* that option. It was because for me, love didn't quit. It was long-suffering and unselfish. In other words, I was never supposed to put myself first if I really loved someone. With the help of this man, I began to see some of the errors in my thought and belief systems. We did everything in our power to try to remain honorable as our feelings for each other grew. We talked fast and often. I worked from home, so there was time to see each other frequently. He made sure I didn't lie to myself about my feelings. He encouraged me to work things out in my marriage despite the fact that I had lost faith in the possibility. I still felt worlds away from my husband, and now everything was complicated by how much I wanted a relationship with this other man.

I separated from my husband just at the time when he was contemplating and verbalizing the possibility that now we might have a real chance to fall in love with each other. I know I seem evil for quitting, but the truth is that my husband broke my heart a hundred times before I broke his. I stood by him for a very long time. I was eager and willing to try. I prayed for us even after I went astray that first time. I still could feel how much I wanted things to get better for us. I remember once when I begged him, cried, was down on my knees asking him to give me something of himself to hang on to. I was married to my husband for about eight years before I ever knew how much he loved his grandfather, and how hurt he was when he died and his parents didn't help him through his grief. All those feelings were hidden in him, and that became the habit of his life. All I ever wanted was gentleness, interest, sharing of joy—to share anything more than the basic and mundane matters of daily living.

I stayed involved with the neighbor for three years after I left my husband. Ultimately, it didn't work out. But I know that we loved each other. There was no question. I know the cost of love now. Part of our demise was due to the fact that I have children—he was younger than I—another problem was that I never felt like I was able to really make him happy, and I tried harder than I should have. I tried to the point of my own detriment and the detriment of my kids. It's that old garbage: You must give everything without a thought to yourself. Lately, I've been putting together an updated version that says when you love, you give everything you can without hurting yourself too much along the way.

The relationship ended in an ugly way. We were coming undone rapidly, and my eye caught someone else's and vice versa. My lover knew of this attraction even before I did. I felt like I had done the most awful thing in the world to have even looked in another direction. I felt like this because I had such high hopes for the relationship. I faulted myself entirely at first. I wanted to get therapy. I thought I was genetically and environmentally incapable of real love. It seemed to me that I was always in love with the possibilities for love. I wanted to be in a dream world where love wasn't just a fairy tale but a fairy tale come true.

Looking back on the relationship that propelled me out of my first marriage, I can say I'm happy now that it happened. Financially, things are difficult right now as a result of it, but I am hoping they won't always be this way. The person I was involved with spent lots of money. He was a serious musician who had the fortune/misfortune of growing up in a well-to-do family and didn't understand the basic costs of life and the proverbial value of a dollar. He spent a lot of money on me and others and showed me how to enjoy a good meal for maybe the first time in my life. I feel guilty because of my kids, though. I want things for them that I can't give them now. Fortunately, their father continues to do well in his business.

I'm also sorry that I wasn't strong enough to get out of my marriage without the help of someone else, and I suffered the complications that went along with that. I do believe that I can finally stand on my own two feet with less fear and more joy. I look at the relationship with my neighbor as my first truly adult relationship, because I was able to bear the consequences of loving. I know I tried my best up until the end, and I felt loved and accepted. It was no small thing to feel truly loved for the first time in my life.

The new relationship I'm in now is slow and sweet and fraught with obstacles. I am in it with my eyes wide open. I don't feel a need to have this man around me all the time. I am grateful when he is with me and confident that when he is, he's mine. He gives to me as best he can—and he has many of his own problems. I am more tolerant and patient. I know that I still have a great deal to do on a personal level. I enjoy my solitude immensely and feel I still don't have enough of it. I enjoy being with the people I love. I've had to relearn that if someone loves me, it doesn't mean that he will or should even attempt to make everything right in my world. Because my relationship with my neighbor had the possibility of being ideal, I was carried away with wanting to do and be everything grand and wonderful for this person and came to expect the same in return. Anything that was regular or typical appeared somehow wrong to me. When I first became involved with my current relationship, I expected my new darling to want to know every last thing about me and try to fix whatever he possibly could. I know now that love means only that you desire to be with someone and share all you can. Love doesn't guarantee any happily-ever-afters. "Now" is the thing that's real, and beyond that is icing. In love, you have the right to expect honesty, trust, kindness, passion, and the best of someone, but you also need to put some of your expectations aside.

I know that I did the right thing to divorce my husband because of the simple fact that we weren't in love. We were as good to each other as possible. We grew a great deal as individuals when we were together. We needed each other at that time in our lives. I'm not certain that his take on all this would be the same as mine. I know that in his heart of hearts, he is aware that he has a severe problem with the emotional world. He is still warm toward me and very good to both me and the kids. He is, thank God, a better father than ever before. He is probably a better father now than I am a mother. I am suffering a bit now but hopeful that change for the better will come.

I made certain to proceed slowly, carefully, and generously with the divorce. I had so much guilt because of the affair. I made an enormous effort to remain friends with my husband because of our children.

I am still slaying my dragons—and I am trying to be careful.

MRS. N

*Mrs. N is sixty years old and has been married to her second
husband for twenty-three years. She lives in a suburb of San Francisco,
works in publicity, is childless, and, over the course of her marriage,
has had several affairs. Yet she admires her husband, has a good sex life
with him, loves his children from a previous marriage, and considers
her nonbiological grandchildren her own. She makes no excuses for her
affairs. She is straightforward and self-effacing. Although she concedes
that the presence of her inattentive father and a period of time in her life
when she suffered from obesity might be psychological culprits in her
pursuit of extramarital affairs, she maintains that the affairs were a
result of her tendency to want more. At this point in her life, she is
content to nest with her husband, leaving the affairs to her memories,
although even at sixty, she never says never again. At the end of the
interview, she laughs and asks, "Am I normal?" "There is no such
thing as normal," we say. She nods gratefully.*

When I married my first husband, I was twenty-four years old and
weighed 220 pounds. When I left my husband three years later, I
weighed 135 pounds, and I'm five foot five, so that was perfect. It was the
first time in my life that I had ever been thin. It was also the first time in my
life that I really can say I lived in the world and wanted to experience all the

things that I hadn't. So many things changed for me during the course of that marriage, not the least of which was my weight. I changed. I became attractive. Suddenly, men found me appealing. I look back on him now and think that my ex-husband was a nice man. I mean, after all, he loved me unconditionally. Truly, all the men I dated after him and during the course of my second marriage, my current marriage, were nice men.

I've had a few affairs. I suppose that sounds rather distasteful—especially since I waited twelve years to remarry, and we had no children to keep us together—but I was spiteful. You see, he decided that we should have a prenuptial agreement, and just a few days before our wedding, he told me about it and asked me to sign. Intellectually, I understood why he wanted it: He had children from a previous marriage and I had none. One of his appealing aspects for me was that he made a lot of money; for him, it was that I had no children. At one point I thought about having children, but it wasn't in my husband's agenda. He'd already had a vasectomy, and I was and am okay with that. I adore my three stepchildren, and we have a wonderful relationship. I couldn't have asked for more if they were my own. This way I don't have the mother baggage, yet I have six wonderful grandchildren, so there's not much more that I could really want.

In retrospect, children would have curtailed my life. I wouldn't have been free to travel. I wouldn't have had the freedom I had in general. It was a trade-off, I suppose, but still, the prenuptial agreement hurt. I was angry.

I was in love with my second husband—very much so—and I still am. Aside from the financial agreement, he represented wonderful things for me. We knew all the same people, and I thought he had a wonderful mind and sense of humor. And he really cared. Some people say that you marry the person you're next to when you want to get married, and it doesn't matter sometimes who that is—it's just that you want to get married—but that wasn't the case with us.

However, life with my husband was emotionally tough. His youngest son was living with us, and although the son and I were very close the first year that my husband and I were dating, once we got married, things changed. I think the boy—he was fourteen then—had all these fantasies about him and his father living in a bachelor pad with cathedral wallpaper, and then I came in and scuttled all those illusions. So my husband's son went to live with his mother. As a grown man, and because hindsight is twenty/twenty, he realizes it was a mistake. The mother was void of emotion. She didn't give him what he needed. She's the kind of woman who should have had grandchildren but not children.

My husband and I had been married only four months when I had the first affair. It was with a gentleman I had met on a plane about five years before my marriage, and every time he came to California, I'd see him. We'd go to dinner and go to bed at the Mark Hopkins Hotel, which was always nice and quite exciting. I suppose I could say it was the result of not only the tension at home vis-à-vis my husband's son, but also because of my anger over the prenuptial agreement. Honestly, though, the affair was exciting. I'm not sure if my husband suspected anything. Part of me believes there was some denial on his behalf. He knew that we had a stormy relationship. We both knew that our marriage was already requiring a lot of work and that the prenuptial agreement had sent all my romantic illusions about marriage straight down the drain. But also, I had lived alone for the previous twelve years and had come and gone as I pleased. In fact, I was never really alone, because I always had a man in my life, although my husband often joked that I lived alone even when I lived with him. In many ways, he was right. He never placed boundaries on me. Had he tried to change my outlook or tried to reel me in, I would have resented him.

Frequently, the assumption about extramarital sex is that the sex at home is not fulfilling. For me, it had nothing to do with that. My sex life with my husband was fulfilling and still is, although my husband is a rather technical and mechanical lover. I could make excuses, as I said before, and say that the affair was born out of anger and out of the fact that I thought I was going to have a ready-made family and then my stepson moved out, but none of that is true. I'm just not big on guilt. You know, I got up this morning and knew that I was going to talk to you about my lovers, and then I thought, Do I really want to schlep all of this stuff up again? And then I decided that yes, I do, I will, and when we finish talking, I'm going to bury it all again.

I'm neither proud nor guilty about my affairs. They were what they were. As time wore on, I wasn't having those affairs in any way to be punitive. I suppose on some level, it was frustration. And the one thing I can tell you is that during the first affair, I spent a lot of time sitting with my best friend on her doorstep and trying to figure it all out. It wasn't because I was guilty—it was more because I wanted to share my feelings about it all with someone else. In many ways, that first year of marriage was a tremendous period of adjustment for me. Hey, you want to hear something strange? I can't remember the guy's name—the first guy. Oh, yeah. Harry. His name was Harry. I was never in love with him. I didn't have a burning desire for him. It was fun. Just plain fun. And it was nice to have the attention.

Since that first affair, I've come to know myself a lot better. I've come to understand some of the things that motivated me. And after therapy and analysis, I can say that I believe it all had something to do with my father. I think that anyone who denies a parental or familial link of some sort to current or past behaviors is either lying or in abject denial. You see, my father was nonexistent for me. He was incapable, for a myriad of reasons, of giving me attention, and although I may understand the reasons now, it doesn't mean that they didn't affect me. My father was not a successful man, and yet my mother was happily married and accepting of him. I think that part of the reason, for her, was that she thought no one else would ever marry her. He was truly a gorgeous man—although he was illiterate—and he was wonderful to her. For me, however, he didn't exist. My guess, in retrospect, is that he was in a terrible depression and, at least to me, simply couldn't give—not because he was withholding but rather because he was incapable. He worked fairly steadily, enough to put food on the table, and that was about it. And obviously, I ate all the food on the table. I reflect on these aspects of my life now and try to understand the attention that I didn't get, and then I think about all the attention I got from different kinds of men.

After Harry, I had an affair with a man I truly cared for—Martin. I knew him from the time before I was married. There was a time when I was dating both Martin and my husband. Martin was divorced, and I was really in love with him, but one day he said, "Listen, I look really good on paper, but don't get too close." He was funny and dynamic and sexy, so we continued the affair. It wasn't so much that he reappeared in my life after I was married but rather that he never left. I probably saw him about two or three times—I'd been married then for about three years. We'd go to his house, which was sweet and charming. Oh, he was such a romantic. Now, it wasn't that my husband wasn't exciting. He was. He is. As I said before, he's a little bit too much of a technical lover. I always said, and I still say, you have to fuck my mind before you can fuck my body, and each one of the men could do that. Each one of them stimulated my mind and taught me something. That was a big element for me. It wasn't all just lust. And yes, my husband stimulated my mind as well, even after we were married. It's just that I wanted *more*. I'd get home around midnight, and my husband wouldn't even ask where I'd been or with whom. Oh, you're looking at me now. You're thinking that maybe the element of inattentiveness in my husband is similar to that in my father. Well, I don't think that's it. I think there was some denial on the part of my husband, but on the other hand, I have to give my husband a lot of credit: I believe that he knew who he got when he got me.

There was never any point when I thought I would leave my husband for any of those men. That wasn't the issue. They were just exciting and I liked them. They were good lovers and that was really it. Sometimes I wonder where Martin is, though. He kind of dropped off the face of the earth. I haven't seen him in about fifteen years. He was very well off, but he had a turbulent life.

There is a bittersweet sidebar to all these stories. When I was single, I went to South America and met a wonderful man. He died a few years ago. His name was Marco, and wow, were we hot and heavy in Brazil. I met Marco in the lobby of a hotel in Rio. I was there with another man at the time and decided to take a walk, and there was Marco and we started talking. He was older than I. A holocaust survivor. He lied about his age, was extraordinarily vain, had been married twice and had more affairs than God. We used to joke that we should just get married, but the truth is that we would have been divorced in five minutes, because we really were so different. But Marco was, I believe, the love of my life. Even after I was married, I would go to Brazil to see Marco, although, strangely enough, I didn't sleep with him anymore. It had nothing to do with any sense of faithfulness to my husband as much as it was that the romantic and sexual aspects of my affair with Marco were over.

I was devastated when Marco died. My husband was very consoling because he had met Marco after he and I were married and he knew the nature of our profound friendship. My husband and Marco got along exceedingly well, although Marco never could figure out how my husband could let me visit despite the fact that at that point, there was no romance. It remained an affair of the heart. You see, Marco *wouldn't* have let me go. I tried to explain that I didn't need my husband's permission and that I would have gone even if he had been opposed to it. I wouldn't have deliberately hurt my husband, but I also wouldn't have allowed him to stop me. And I think my husband knew that he couldn't stop me, so it was a moot point. You see, my husband has given me what I've needed. He always gave me my freedom, and I took it. He never put restraints on me; whether he knew or had an idea or any thoughts about my extramarital affairs is something I will never know. If he did, he never expressed them. Some may call that neglect. If that's neglect, then I like that kind of neglect.

I don't think it's a matter of who loves whom more in my marriage. My marriage has evolved to what it is today, and we both married for different reasons. Along with love, I wanted security when I married him. I think he wanted somebody who would do all the things that I used to do for him. He wanted someone to take care of him. You see, he would say, "Jump!" and I would say, "How high and how many somersaults?" But that's not who I am today.

I'm trying to remember the other affairs. I think there were probably four or five. I am very attracted to Israeli men, and there was a man I met in Jerusalem when my husband and I were there on vacation. It was an absolute coming together for the two of us, but it never did work out. I was good friends with his wife. Something easily could have happened one night when his wife wasn't home, but I told him that the one thing I don't do is fuck in another woman's bed. A hotel would have been another thing, but that I couldn't do once I became friends with his wife. I still think about him sometimes, since we never consummated our relationship. I wonder sometimes if we might still get together . . . who knows? Maybe next week.

I had a one-minute affair with someone I flirted with for a year or so. One day we consummated the relationship, and that was, forgive the pun, a real anticlimax. He was a technical lover. The talk and the fantasy were a lot more exciting that the reality. Another time I was at a private piano recital at the home of a very wealthy dowager in Marin County. A Russian—I can't remember his name—was very appealing, then his friend came over and was even more appealing. I remember his friend had on Gucci shoes, and that added to his appeal. I loved the flirtation, not to mention that he was interesting and entrepreneurial and very sexual. We had an affair before he went back to Paris, and then I went to Paris and saw him there, and then he came back and I saw him again and did some work for his company. Then I lost his phone number and spent years wanting to know how he was. It had nothing to do with the sexual end of it, really. I suppose he could have reached me as well, but he was married and estranged from his wife and living with another woman. Complicated, to say the least.

There was no need for justification on the parts of my lovers or myself. They were what they were. They were merely another part of my life, another chapter. You know what? I just remembered someone else. I had a long affair with him, two to three years. He was an executive and a powerful man, but slight, and I don't usually care for little men, because I feel like I dwarf them. He was integral in my learning process: exciting and quirky. We were hot and heavy. He wasn't married.

Maybe one person here and there knew about my affairs over the years. My best friend knew. You see, they weren't conquests. And with the people I told, I never felt judged. The only advice I was given was to be careful. I suppose that I worried about getting caught to some extent, a small extent. Maybe that was denial on my part. Maybe I just didn't want to admit that it was worrisome. My husband never confronted me, and I never thought about what I would do if he did. I have a tendency to stick my head in the sand if I don't want to deal with things. I figure eventually, I'll pull out my head and then all the unpleasant stuff will have gone away.

The last time I had an affair was about ten years ago, and in the interim there was a kind of mind-fucking with my friend in Jerusalem. I don't speak to him regularly anymore, but when I saw him last spring, there was still a sort of electricity. I would rather be flirtatious at this point. Affairs aren't necessary for me anymore. It's like choosing not to have sugar: I know what it tastes like; I've sampled it; so do I want to go back and taste another brownie when they all taste pretty much alike? Maybe one sweet is a little bit more superb than another, and I have had some wonderful relationships, both sexually and cerebrally. I am who I am because of them, but affairs no longer feed me the way they used to. To be perfectly honest, a great deal has to do with body image. I don't look the way I did at thirty or forty or even fifty. Would I today, this minute, have an affair if somebody walked into my life? No. My body is not in the best of shape, and that would bother me. It would take a lot of mind-fucking for me to go to bed with someone. I love banter, and the banter is more fun at this point. I am working with someone who was very appealing when I first met him. I adore his wife—although that's not the issue—I just feel that our business relationship is much better and more valuable than going to bed with him.

Also, I don't know if I want to do this to my husband anymore. We have worked real hard to achieve the relationship we have and, well, been there, done that. Funny, my husband is short and chubby and bald, and that has always been the type of man to whom I've been attracted. Maybe it's my own sense of self-worth that tells me I could never get the tall, dark, and handsome movie star, but I find that type insipid. I want substance, not great looks. I feel that the not-pretty men have more depth—well, not all of them, but I've just never been attracted to pretty men. My best friend always said when we walk down the street and we see two disparate men, "There's yours and there's mine." She goes for the pretty boys.

Maybe it's not only that I don't want to do this to my husband but also that I have cultivated more respect for myself. I don't want to put myself out there anymore. Maybe I am more aware. Maybe I think more of my husband now. Maybe I don't want to risk hurting him, and I also feel that I have more to lose. Primarily, I don't want to do this anymore. None of the relationships were painful because I never thought I'd leave my husband and be taken away on a white horse. There was no longing when I wasn't with these men, simply a strong desire when I was with them. Sometimes I wonder how they are and how their children and grandchildren are—they're like good friends whom I happened to sleep with.

I don't think my husband was ever unfaithful. I don't think it was necessary for him in the way it was for me. I'd be surprised if he was and more upset to find out where and when in our relationship it happened. I would hope to think that in the last five or six years, nothing happened, because we've worked hard. You see, my affairs had nothing to do with his personality; they only had to do with mine. For me, the affairs were exciting. The attention was appealing, and I still get it today, but in a different way, from the men around me.

I used to think that for my fiftieth birthday, I would have liked a party with all the men in my life. I would have wanted everyone to know why they were really there. By the time I was fifty-five, I wanted just women to come to a luncheon. It changes for us, and I'm not sure where or why or how, but one day you just wake up and say, "I'd rather have my women friends to lunch than men or just a man." It's not that I don't still want to have lunch with men. Recently, I had to address a focus group of about 150 men, and I was quite flirtatious and enjoyed every minute of it. I hadn't felt that way in a long time, and it was exhilarating.

Sometimes I think part of me is still open to having an affair, although it would be more difficult, of course. It would have to be something that I really wanted, and at this point, I would rather just spend three or four afternoons talking. It's like what I always said, "Fuck my mind first and then you can fuck my body." Yet it's different for me now. I doubt that my mind has meant as much to the men as theirs meant to me. I have no illusions. I'm a realist. But they gave me all the mental stimulation that I needed, and I gave them what they needed. Sure, they might have just settled for the sexual— I'm a good lover—but they were lucky they got the whole package.

I'm nesting more now. My husband and I do our own thing, but we also spend time together. He works the weekends sometimes, and I do errands. We often have friends over or go to someone's house or just stay at home and watch television. We don't fight. We never fought. My husband has a temper, but now he takes medication for that, and it's amazing what medication can do for anger. He's very complex. He is a true Renaissance man—

he acts, he plays piano, writes, plays guitar. He probably shouldn't be a probate lawyer—it's so dry, and he's very interesting. I always kid him about all the things he knows and ask where he learned them. I don't know when he found the time. Those qualities in my husband are what drew me to him in the first place, but it's just that I've always needed and wanted more.

MRS. O

*Mrs. O is a tall, good-looking woman in her fifties with a
wholesome country demeanor. From a wealthy and well-known
southern family, she is not only a former actress and model but a
Ph.D. professor at a major university in the South. She is also palpably
sexually charged, with one thing on her mind: pleasure. Although she
thought her husband was exactly the man she was looking for when
she married, he was far from Mr. Right. He made both her and
their children miserable. He provided many materialistic things but
wasn't the Prince Charming she'd thought. In the beginning, it
appeared that the relationship she entered into outside her marriage
was the one that truly satisfied her. In the end, she concluded sadly
that both her husband and her lover had let her down. Fortunately, her
children are grown and have gone unscathed. Now she is divorced and
lonely and harbors many regrets.*

I had the affair because of me, not anyone else. I felt at the time I needed
more from the marriage, so I decided to go outside of my marriage to find
happiness.

Shortly after we were married, my husband became very cold. Although
he was affectionate in the beginning, the warmth went by the wayside a few
years later. He became the stereotypic workaholic. Time spent with me and

the kids was perfunctory. He was, although a decent father, undemonstrative. As for our marriage, what had once felt right and easy became a chore. Even our sex life became monotonous: At the beginning of the marriage, there was a lot of foreplay, and I got a lot of attention, which made me happy, but when that changed and he changed, I sought affection from someone else. I couldn't understand the change in my husband.

I love to dance. My husband didn't like to dance, so I'd go out to clubs with girlfriends. I met a guy one night. I was sitting at the bar, drinking margaritas, having a good time. He offered to buy me a drink. We started talking, and I was physically attracted to him from the moment he sat down.

He was so different from my husband. I was so attracted to him. From the moment we met, I knew we would end up, you know, together. It was a big mistake. I swear, I didn't go out looking for someone. Although I was unhappy, I hadn't dressed provocatively. All I wanted to do was dance a little and have some fun, but deep down inside, perhaps I was deceiving myself as to what it was I really wanted.

After the first night with my lover, I climbed into bed, and my husband just screwed me. It was so cold. Imagine! And after I'd had that wonderful evening at my lover's apartment. I wanted to tell my husband how I felt. He was once my friend, but I felt I could no longer talk to him at all. He made me feel so empty. I wanted to tell him to love me and to feel me; "make love to me" were the words that I wanted to say, but I knew the love was gone.

In the long run, the affair didn't help my marriage, not at all. Eventually, my husband found out. He actually called my mom to ask her to plead with me to stay and not break up our home for this guy. My whole family was upset with me. Everyone tried to get me not to leave, but I had a mind of my own, and I was miserable in the marriage, so of course I left. People thought I was crazy, but I'd made up my mind. My ex-husband and I never talked about why I wanted to leave. I just wanted out, so I filed for divorce, and I made my boyfriend file for divorce from his wife right away.

I actually thought I'd found Prince Charming outside my marriage. What a fool I was. I really don't know what I was thinking. I yearned for a fantasy world where everything was perfect and my life would be the fairy tale. I thought, My goodness, I've found a wonderful person in this life who is perfect, perfect in every way, or so I thought in my make-believe fantasy world.

I moved in with my lover. Later, and so ironically, I found out that my husband had been cheating on me as well, and that was one of the reasons he had become so cold and distant. I had no idea he was cheating when I decided to have my affair. I think if my husband had stayed the way he was when we first got married, we'd still be together. I am still very attracted to him, even now. He has remarried several times.

It's been almost twenty-seven years since the divorce. We were married in 1969. Once we split and I moved in with my lover, a lot of horrible things happened: My two kids, five and seven at the time, came with me, although my son later went to live with his father because he was so unhappy living with me and my boyfriend.

When I left my comfortable lifestyle, I found out that my boyfriend had nothing, none of the things I thought he had or that he'd told me he had. I remember listening to the waves, which had sounded so romantic on our many magical nights, and thinking that now they sounded like rocks hitting up against a brick wall.

I knew at that point there was nothing romantic about my new situation, but I went ahead with it anyway. Things got progressively worse. For one thing, my lover started using drugs. He would start arguing about nothing just so I would react. Yet I was totally faithful to him the whole time we were together. He traveled a lot for his job, and he seemed to be gone more and more. One day he came home and announced he wouldn't be back again. This wonderful, passionate, fantasy love affair dried up and fizzled away. To think that I thought he was what I had always longed and hoped for. I believe he wanted to give me reasons to leave him. And he did. In the end, my daughter and I had to move in with my mom. And then my ex sent for my daughter because we couldn't make it.

I moved out of my fabulous, well-appointed, beautiful million-dollar home to be with a deadbeat drug-addicted boyfriend who I thought was The Answer. I thought I was in love. What can I say? I look back on things and think I must have been crazy. I really must have lost my mind. What in the world was I thinking?

It was so painful breaking up the family the way I did. It was devastating. I really wish I'd stayed. I wish I'd kept my family together. I should have worked harder at my marriage. I should have tried to understand my ex-husband more. I knew what I had. If I were a bigger and stronger person, I would have tried to understand what was going on and tried to make it work, but I was selfish, that's what it boils down to. I was selfish and only took care of my needs. I didn't consider his needs, nor did I consider the family's needs.

I think people should think long and hard about having an affair. In retrospect, I don't recommend it. There is no circumstance I can think of that would warrant having an affair. If you feel you want to have an affair, then it's time to go. It's too risky. Go, before you destroy several lives as well as your own. There's no room for a third party in a marriage.

MRS. P

In her late thirties, Mrs. P is a physician living in a suburb in Michigan who never wanted to have an affair. She was married to a blue-collar worker and loved him madly, but when he lost his job, his self-esteem plummeted. He physically and emotionally abused her. She's convinced that one of the reasons he tortured her was his jealousy because she was educated and he was not. A macho guy, he couldn't bear the thought that she was the breadwinner. She did everything: worked every day at her office, came home and took care of the kids, and had sex with him every night. She had two children— one she had as an unwed teenager, and one with her husband. An affair was the furthest thing from her mind.

When we met, ours was the most unlikely coupling ever. I was doing my medical residency and worked so hard that there was no time to socialize, and definitely no time for a marriage. I'd had a child when I was sixteen, so I graduated from medical school late because I was getting myself together again. It was tough being a single mom and all, but I have to thank my family for helping me see this life's goal through. I'd wanted to be a doctor since I was a little kid, but I also had a hefty sexual appetite when I was young.

I had sex for the first time when I was thirteen and couldn't stop after that. I remember coming home once at fifteen, drunk and half dressed, and my parents didn't even say anything, so I thought it was okay. That was the night I conceived my son in the backseat of a car. At the time I thought I was in love. No one can possibly know what love is at fifteen.

Eventually, I was able to meet someone whom I loved and who, in the beginning at least, wasn't in competition with me. He had a good job, he worked nine to five, and that was fine with me as well. I needed someone to help balance my life. He wanted a child of his own, and I agreed that as soon as I could get into a residency program, I would be willing to try again. Even though my first child was a teenager by the time I married, I wanted to give him a stable, happy family, and my husband was good to him. My husband was always there for my son. He shuttled him around to guitar lessons and tutors, which took a lot of the pressure off my parents. While I pursued my career, I relied a great deal on my parents to look after my son. When my parents retired, they moved in with us. It was cheaper and more convenient, especially since I needed the support. When my husband and I got married and he moved in with us, the situation with my parents became tense. I thought everyone seemed okay with the arrangements, but they really weren't. To my mind, my son had a great role model, we had my parents, and I felt comfortable leaving for the hospital and office at ridiculous hours.

The sex in my marriage was good in the beginning, but not great. It was loving and comfortable, at times a little wild, but mostly, it was fine. Since I was gone most of the time, it was hard to have a lot of time alone anyway. We could have had a bit more sexual diversity, but I wasn't even thinking about it. I was so happy that my son and I had found a great man. Little else mattered.

Everything was going along well until one day I came home in the middle of the day to get some rest before going back to the office, and I found my husband home in his pajamas, asleep in my parents' bed. They were away in Hilton Head for the winter. I thought that was strange and woke him up, thinking he wasn't feeling well. He was a bit shocked when he saw me, but he hugged me and encouraged me to join him. I asked what was going on, and he explained that his company had been laying off people at the plant and that his hours had been reduced. I wanted to know how long this had been going on. He told me it had happened a few days before, and hopefully, things would be picking up soon and he'd get more hours. I later found out this was a lie, but I was too exhausted not to believe him. I set the alarm clock, lay down in my parents' bed, and we took a nap together.

When I woke up, he was still asleep. I kissed him and headed back out to work. I got home late that night and the house was very dark. Dirty dishes were all over the house, his clothes were thrown all over the place, and he and my son were playing video games in the basement. This irritated me, but I let it go because I figured he might have been depressed about having his hours reduced at his job, and I didn't want to further upset him. The job market was tough. He seemed very tense. Our relationship was becoming the kind in which we really didn't talk anymore—and didn't talk about what the issues were.

I don't think it had anything to do with our differences in education. He appeared to be an angry man who lost his job and was having a hard time. Problem was, he didn't even go out looking for another one. He stayed at home—eating, drinking, and hanging out with his friends. He took care of my child, but that was a major thing between us, because he was always throwing it back in my face. He got very drunk one night and angrily yelled at me, saying that my son wasn't his child and he didn't have any responsibility. He called me a whore and told me I was irresponsible. Well, that was the last straw—and by then we'd had a child together.

I loved my husband, but that was before all of the abuse. He struck me in front of my child, and I was completely devastated. We were at war by then, and I needed real help from the outside. He was abusive, and I wasn't going to take it. I'd felt so secure with him until then. Now I feel as though I never knew who he really was. Our lives were in complete turmoil. Suddenly, I was a hardworking woman trying to raise children and instill some good values in them. He was a person with a violent temper, no self-esteem, and no job. It was all too incendiary.

Very soon after the abuse started, I ran out of the house, taking my children with me. One of the guards let us stay in the residency ward at the hospital. My husband came down to the hospital looking for us. He was drunk and threatening everyone. I was so embarrassed, I couldn't even think straight. The guard at the gate called to say that my husband was there, being very loud, and was possibly under the influence of some type of drugs. He also had a weapon.

We were protected because the guard would not let him in. We stayed overnight and were petrified. I didn't know what to do so finally, I called my parents in Hilton Head and asked them to come for us. I told them there was an emergency and I cried into the phone. They, of course, made airline reservations immediately. No one was going to treat their daughter and grandchildren that way.

My husband and I reconciled, but I knew I couldn't make love to him again. I worked to put our marriage back together, but it was a farce. I supported him and took care of him, but he had no ambition. He had become a drug addict and alcoholic.

I started having an affair with the guard who had protected us that night. I worked the night shift, so we stayed together and kept a nice romantic relationship going for years. My husband was becoming more of a nightmare as the days wore on. He stole from us. He wouldn't get a job. He wouldn't leave the house. The only happiness I found was with my lover. The relationship was so innocent and special. My mom knew about the affair, and although she didn't condone it with words, there was silence that said she understood. My father told me I had to keep my marriage together and encouraged me to get help for my husband.

At that point, however, I was so through with my husband and my marriage. I didn't care what he did at that point. All I knew was that I wanted out. Ultimately, my husband ended up getting arrested and was sent to jail. I was very thankful, because if he hadn't been, he may have killed us. He was really a mess, so bitter and angry. Our relationship had been over for a long time. I kept it going because I was afraid of him.

I thought I knew my husband better than I did, but I obviously didn't. He turned out to be a savage. To think that I trusted him with my children because I was so happy to have someone in my life who cared about me. I overlooked all the signals that screamed caution. He met me when I was at my all-time low and he still fell in love with me. I believed in him, but I should have seen the writing on the wall.

Once my husband was convicted and sent away, my relationship with the guard became public. He remains the most sensitive person. He's always known just how to treat me and how bruised I'd been from that violent situation.

I'm divorced now. My ex-husband has kept in touch with both children (from his jail cell), and we're trying to schedule visitations. I've learned how to love with my new man. It is the relationship that I was looking for all along. Although I cheated on my husband with my lover, who is now my husband, he knew what the circumstances were and what I was going through. He was right there through it all. I love him and am not afraid anymore.

I don't consider what I had an affair; it was a relationship of survival. I loved my husband but realized he didn't love himself, and he took that out on me. I did what I was supposed to do, and he couldn't deal with that. He had issues with my job and what I did for a living, but I wanted him to know my job was what I did, not who I was.

My new husband and I are planning a family and want to make a nice home for my two children. My oldest is heading off to college, where he's enrolled in a premed program. He wants to follow in my footsteps. He had a hard time dealing with the violence and abuse in my first marriage, and I am grateful that the story has a happy ending.

I am so happy now, although I wouldn't advise anyone to have an affair. However, I don't think my first marriage was a real marriage. It was more like playing house—in a house of cards.

MRS. Q

Mrs. Q is a Latin-American woman living in the Midwest who, earlier in her life, was interested in two things: landing a husband and being a stay-at-home mom. Ironically, it was her frustration with trying to get pregnant that drove her to have an affair. Additionally, she says that as a woman of Latin heritage, she couldn't imagine having sex with just one man for the rest of her life. She confesses that she went on to higher education—she has a master's degree in business—only because she believed her mother's advice that attending school was the best way to meet an educated, ambitious, well-to-do man. Now in her forties, she has no interest in working and is still trying to conceive a child with her husband.

I was very young when I married, only twenty-two. Even though I already had my master's degree, I had a hard time getting a job, so I became a housewife, which was my goal anyway. I admit, I was lazy about looking for a job. I had worked very hard in school and really needed a break. I didn't tell my husband that. He thought I was looking for a job every day, so I lied just a little. The truth is, I wanted it to appear that I was interested in a career, but I wasn't.

At first it was fine. We lived in the city, and I had all the luxuries at my fingertips. I could order an elegant dinner and have it delivered. I could play tennis outside in the park during the warmer months and be ready for my handsome husband when he arrived home. I had the good life, loved my husband, and was eager to be a good wife.

I managed to get away with the leisurely life for close to three years. I kept my brain stimulated by reading everything I could get my hands on and by helping out in my husband's investment-banking firm from time to time. I read all of the pertinent periodicals—The New York Times, USA Today, The Financial Times, and Crain's. I didn't want to miss a word. It allowed me to go out with my husband and his colleagues and not sound like some housewife without a brain. Other housewives sounded so brainless to me, and I wanted no part of that. After all, I was educated, but I had no interest in a real job.

Working at my husband's office once or twice a month occupied me, but I was getting very bored. I figured it was time to get pregnant. I tried that for months, and months turned into a year, so I went to a specialist. I was certain there was something wrong. I mean, I was only twenty-six: Why wasn't I getting pregnant? When I was a teenager, I got pregnant easily. I started to worry that maybe I wasn't conceiving because of the several abortions I'd had in my youth.

We tried and tried to conceive. Our bedroom turned into a laboratory. I took my temperature fifteen days after my period started. There were all kinds of ovulation tests, pregnancy tests, thermometers, and pills on the nightstand. We had to make sure we had sex at the right time of day or night, even in the middle of the night. I traveled to meet my husband, sometimes across the country, if the time was right to have sex. I was getting frustrated and restless. Our sex life sucked. There was no more spontaneity. We had sex only when we needed to in order to conceive. Eight years went by, and we were getting rather bored with each other. We went to therapists in attempts to rekindle the passion. Then my husband began to suffer the inability to perform, and I suffered the frustration of trying to have a fulfilling sex life.

I needed some attention.

True, I became obsessed with trying to get pregnant, and the situation was getting a little out of hand. Between the lab in the bedroom, his impotence, and my neediness, things were at an all-time low.

I felt that I was looking old. My face was sagging. The once-fine lines had turned into crevices. I thought it was sun damage from all of the vacations we took when we tried to get some romance going, or to relax, but it was from worry and angst about my marriage and my life. I had always been pretty shapely and sexy, and I felt that I was becoming a real dumpy chick. I also had a strong sense that my husband was cheating. I felt that his impotence was a lack of desire for me, and perhaps a result of all the trying to have a baby. It became a vicious cycle: I didn't even want my husband, and I was overcome with guilt and frustration because I couldn't have a baby.

One day I was at work in my husband's office. I ran for the elevator, and there was a gorgeous, very well-dressed black man standing there. He looked like a black Clark Gable. He was absolutely stunning, and I couldn't stop staring at him. Even though I felt that I was looking so frumpy—my hair was tied back in a bun; I was wearing thick ugly glasses and a long ugly plaid skirt and flat shoes—he looked at me as though he wanted to eat me alive. I loved the attention.

We started to talk about mundane subjects like the weather, what floor I worked on, and so on, and he asked me if I was free for lunch the next day. I said that I was, even though I actually had plans. I asked him to meet me in the cafeteria. Well, one thing led to another at the cafeteria, and lunch turned into dinner. I never even got to my workout that day.

Our lunch had been a quick salad and iced tea, and he invited me to his apartment, which was a short distance away. I assumed correctly that he was married, because women's things were all over his apartment. I told him that I, too, was married, and it seemed to relieve the tension.

He reassured me that his wife was traveling on business and she wouldn't be coming home for a week. I'd noticed some lab kits in their bathroom and asked if they'd had any kids. He told me they were trying, but there had been some problems. He didn't think it was him, but he wanted to try at least once more to have the child that he'd wanted all his life. He told me how the whole lab thing was such a turnoff, and that he felt he was having sex not for pleasure but because it was the right time of the month. His wife had told him that he couldn't masturbate for three days before she ovulated because the "good" sperm had to build up. He told me their sex life had become a nightmare, more of a means to an end rather than an act of love or passion. It sounded all too familiar.

We made love on the floor in his guest room. The sex was amazing. He knew exactly what to do. We made love into the evening. I called my husband and told him I was having dinner with friends.

I knew I had to leave, but I didn't want to go home. I wanted to be with this man all night. He was so passionate and honest. I dressed myself, still with the scent of sex on my skin. I had to get into my house and get cleaned up before my husband suspected anything.

Luckily, he had dinner with a friend that night and wasn't home when I arrived. I pulled my clothes off and sank into a hot bubbly bath and stared into space. I felt so lost and empty. I sat in that tub for nearly an hour, just lost in thought, until I realized that my skin was wrinkly and the water was cold. I had so many thoughts racing around my head. Having sex with that man had almost emptied my soul. I'd broken my commitment to my husband for immediate gratification, and I felt lower than I'd ever felt before. I wanted kids so badly. I don't know what made me go outside of my marriage to find comfort. I felt so needy.

I heard my husband coming in the door and knew I had to pull myself together. I'd been crying and didn't want it to show. My emotions were so raw.

My husband came upstairs and kissed me. He went to get into bed and said he would wait up for me, but fortunately, he was a little tipsy and had passed out on the bed before I could even dry off. I kissed him good night and vowed to myself that I would never again look outside of the marriage for comfort or sex. Suddenly, I loved my husband and wanted to make our relationship work. I didn't want to be without him and realized I loved him more than ever.

When he woke up the next morning, I nursed him back from his hangover. We talked endlessly about committing ourselves to having a baby. It had been almost nine years. We made a promise that we'd try for another six months, and if it didn't happen within that time period, we would consider adoption or live our lives committed to each other without children.

I saw my lover only that one time. As wonderful as it had been to be with him, I knew I couldn't see him anymore, because I never wanted to feel that emptiness again. Maybe the affair drove me back to my husband and made me love him even more, but I wish that rekindling could have been accomplished in another way. I felt that I stooped too low to get some relief.

I do not recommend having an affair to anyone. If you get to a point where you think that cheating is the answer, stop yourself and try to imagine the emptiness you might well feel when it's over. I mean, you can't be with that person anyway, except physically, and all of your emotions are at stake. Please think twice, three times, or more before you do anything like this. If you do have an affair and find that you still love your husband, tell him, confess, and then swear to yourself that you will never do it again. That was the hardest part, but I was lucky: When I told my husband the truth, he still embraced me.

To this day, I think about my lover and the physical pleasure he gave me. It was magical.

Mrs. R

ର୍ଯ

Mrs. R lives in North Carolina. In her late thirties, she's a tall, curly-haired bleached blonde with a shapely figure. She grew up in a family on the proverbial wrong side of the tracks and spent much of her childhood riding from her part of town to the part where beautiful homes abounded. Her mother worked for a wealthy family as a house manager and encouraged her daughter to educate herself, asserting that higher education was the one place where she was sure to meet a man. Mrs. R went to law school; she was determined not only to meet a "good husband" but to realize her childhood dream of living in one of the beautiful homes. She met a guy while studying in the law library, had a high-society wedding, and then started cheating a year into their marriage. They've been married for twenty years, and she is, for lack of a better term, a serial cheater. Her defense when it comes to her infidelity is her feeling that it saved her marriage. Despite the passion of the affairs, the anxiety made her want to go home to her husband— and stay there.

The truth is, I have always had bad relationships with men because I was raped when I was eleven. I haven't told anyone about the rape until now, not even my husband or my mother. I feel that it is an important fact in my story, since my sexuality was exposed when I was so young. Unquestionably, the rape colored the way I viewed sex until much later in life. In my younger years, and even through the better part of my marriage, I never equated sex with love. Sex was simply about sex. It was merely a physical outlet for me, and I became quite proficient. Being good at sex far outweighed the aspects of sexual expression that had to do with passion and love.

I married my husband because he was the "right" guy, from both social and financial points of view, and the sex was good at best—not great, but good enough. I don't know if I ever really loved my husband, but I cared for him and felt that marrying him would change my life for the better. Marrying him was all about doing the right thing and creating the right life. I also knew, not too far in the back of my mind, that he wouldn't be the last man I would screw.

My husband is six years younger than I, although he never found out until we went to get the marriage license. He was upset because I'd lied to him. But I had correctly anticipated his reaction, and that was why I lied: He was also concerned that our chances for having children would be diminished because of my age. Had I confessed my age sooner, he might not have married me. Really, the age difference wasn't so bad: I was thirty and he was twenty-four. Besides, I felt much younger than thirty and looked like a kid. We were happy, or perhaps I should say I was happy, for about a year, until I got restless.

As I said, the sex was good, but I needed more. I wanted to get a little freaky, and when I dropped a few hints to my husband along those lines, he got disgusted with me. I knew I wasn't getting the gratification of imaginative sex at home, so I backed off, stopped asking, and figured I'd find it someplace else.

Shortly after that, I met a guy, an engineer who was visiting one of the partners in my office. The partners invited me to lunch with them and the engineer, and I couldn't take my eyes off him. I flirted with him all through lunch. Just as I was writing down my number for him, he asked for it. My coworkers told him that I was married. He was married, too. He'd read all my signals. Apparently, he knew precisely what he was doing, and I knew what I was doing as well.

He called. We met for drinks, and too many drinks and a puff on a joint led me to his apartment and amazing sex. I didn't bother to call my husband and say I'd be coming home late. When I got home late that night, I tiptoed in the door, showered, and crawled into bed beside my snoring husband.

When he woke up the next morning, he wanted to screw. I certainly didn't feel like it, but I did it without a second thought. As I said, sex could be pretty much rote for me. Despite the other man, I was determined to keep my marriage together. I'll never forget that morning when my husband kissed me as he left for work: On the one hand, I felt guilty, but on the other, my husband was beginning to make me sick. He just turned me off. He called at the end of the day and said he wanted us to take a romantic weekend in the islands, so he booked a long weekend in the Caymans. All I wanted to do that day was get back with my lover.

After that first time, I wanted sex with my lover all the time. I had sex with my husband when I had to—dutifully, perfunctorily. There was no doubt in my mind that the trip to the Caymans was going to make me miserable, but I knew I had to go in order to sustain my marriage. My lover and I had sex the day before, and that weekend, all I could think about was my lover.

I stayed with my lover for about four years, until I got pregnant with my first child. I knew I was carrying my husband's baby because my lover and I always used a condom and my husband and I had unprotected "married" sex.

We welcomed our first daughter, and I stopped seeing my lover. I knew I had to cool it with the extramarital affair, and my lover cared enough about me to step aside when it was clearly time to call it quits. The relationship ended naturally and easily. There was no drama.

For a while, my marriage became normal, until I started to get bored and restless again. Sex with my husband was fine, but I still felt the need for something different. My hormones must have been raging, because I felt even sexier than before I had my child. I stopped working after I had the baby, as I had planned all along, and that placed a bit of a strain on the relationship, since my husband didn't want his friends to think that his wife was just a "housewife." He wanted to be married to a career woman. Despite the modicum of tension—my not working and a new baby—we still had sex a few times a month, and things remained status quo.

I was coming out of my gym class one day and noticed this guy. We talked for a while. I didn't want to do anything, so I left abruptly and went home, but I couldn't stop thinking about him. Since I had one child and knew I'd probably eventually have another, I wasn't looking for someone else. I was afraid of temptation. I was a mother. I couldn't let the cheating go on. The adventure had to end.

I hugged my beautiful baby daughter when I got home that afternoon and tried to keep myself distracted. I played with her and read stories, but it was impossible to stop thinking about that other man. My conflict and frustration left me crying out loud and screaming when I was alone. I didn't want to have an affair again, but I wasn't sure I could keep myself from having another affair. I'd been married about nine years—what was I thinking?

I didn't go to my gym class for weeks. I was really trying to stay away. One day I broke down and went. I knew what I was risking, but I went anyway. He was there and told me that he'd been to class every single day, hoping he'd see me. He asked me out for lunch again, and that time I couldn't resist. Everything was going along just fine, and then he asked the question: "Are you married?" I told him I was and that I was happy. He questioned me about my happiness as he visually undressed me. I didn't have that much on anyway, since we'd just finished the class. I got weak and started to feel nauseated. He leaned over and kissed me on the lips, just a peck, but it sent me soaring. I really wanted to have sex with him.

We went to his apartment and made unbelievably erotic love all afternoon. I fell asleep, and when I woke up, it was nighttime and I had eight messages on my cell phone. I panicked and realized that it was past the time for my babysitter to leave. There was a great deal of friction between the babysitter and me, so when I later learned that she'd asked my mother-in-law to come stay with my daughter, I wasn't surprised. The sitter never even attempted to reach me on my cell phone. She knew that my husband was at a trial and couldn't leave work.

When I got home, my mother-in-law just stared at me. There I was, still in my gym clothes from that morning. No makeup. Hair undone. I was quite a sight. I lied and told her I had passed out at the gym and they had to call 911, but she knew I was lying. When she left, she turned to me and said, "Don't fuck up!" I was both in shock and mortified. To her credit, she never said anything to anybody, even though I am certain she knew exactly what I was up to. My husband never said anything, either. He never asked any questions. He was simply concerned that I wasn't feeling well. Shortly after that, I found out that I was pregnant again. This time I freaked out, although my lover and I had used protection. Our son was born, and everyone said he looked just like every single dead relative on my husband's side, so I felt a bit of relief.

I knew this had to stop. That I had to stop. The last affair had taken years off my life. I promised myself I wouldn't sleep around anymore. I resigned myself to fantasy and frustration. About a year after my son was born, I had another baby girl. Although I vowed not to have another affair, I did have two more brief affairs after our third child was born.

In my own defense, those affairs kept me sane and helped me stay with my husband. They kept me whole. In strange ways, they helped me to understand what a loving relationship was and could be. Ultimately, I have grown into a loving relationship with my husband. I finally realized that although sex was not as exciting with my husband as it had been with the lovers, it was much more important to have a man who loved and adored me and would do anything for me. All I was doing was having anonymous sex for physical pleasure.

I've sort of settled into the life that I've chosen. We've been married about twelve years now, and we're happy. I am a stay-at-home mom. This is what I always dreamed of being. My husband is an extremely successful lawyer with a very large corporation. I had one more conversation with my mother-in-law about the incident, and although she was cold toward me, she never let on that she knew or that she ever even suspected. Since that day I came home late in my gym clothes, our relationship has been cordial but definitely cool, restrained and distant.

There is no question in my mind that the rape altered and warped my view of my own sexuality. I don't recommend affairs unless the purpose is a last resort to save a marriage, and I do believe that can be a bona fide and justifiable reason. Having an affair during the childbearing years can cause a great deal of anxiety. Potential complications (like not knowing whose baby you are carrying) could change and damage your life forever. If you're going to have an affair, be discreet. Remember that you always run the risk of destroying your marriage and possibly a family.

MRS. S

Mrs. S is in her late forties and living in the Boston area with her
third husband and a child from a previous relationship. She works
catch-as-catch-can. She became pregnant by her lover while married to
her second husband, which ultimately dissolved that marriage. After
concluding that the baby wasn't his, her second husband ostracized her
and made her life miserable. In each of her marriages, cheating on her
part or the part of her husband was always the primary reason for
getting divorced. The child is ten now.

I was married for the first time at twenty-three. I honestly believed it was
for keeps. My first husband was an insurance broker who had his own
business, and although we lived on a very meager income, I enjoyed being
his wife. The sex was amazing, and we spent long hours pleasing each other,
exploring each other's bodies and making each other truly happy and satisfied.

We had a nice life together, and although I had no career aspirations (I
worked in an upscale department store), I enjoyed making a home for my
husband. Things went along well for us for about seven years. I really think
he may have been my soul mate. I was convinced that since we spent so
much time with each other, there would never be room in our marriage for

even the threat of someone else. We talked about having kids, but it wasn't a priority. He didn't earn that much in his small insurance business, but business was picking up, and coupled with my salary, we weren't doing too badly. We were so happy, and I felt that our lives were complete. We never used protection, and I sort of wondered why I didn't get pregnant; I mean, there was no way I missed having sex on a day I was ovulating.

My husband came home one day and announced that he had received a job offer from an insurance company in Miami. I had to start thinking about where we were going to live and how I would be able to transfer to the local store. We had started the fertility process, but I figured there would be doctors in Miami who might even have a different diagnosis. We moved to a large, well-appointed apartment that overlooked the beach in Boca Raton. Things seemed perfect, and we were still having sex several times a week, even though we'd been married five years. My husband started wondering what was going on.

Little did I know that his consternation regarding my inability to conceive was because he had recently fathered a child with his mistress. As a matter of fact, I didn't know about his mistress and his child until a year after his baby's birth, when I discovered that his mistress lived across town from us in Miami. Needless to say, he and I never conceived. I filed for divorce, living in a place where I knew no one, and I determined to start a new life.

I met a seemingly wonderful man who really wasn't my type but wanted to get married and have kids right away. I told him I wanted kids more than anything. He had been married before—three times—but didn't have children, so I was eager to get things going. I continued with the fertility treatments, although I didn't mention them to my new husband. I didn't see any reason to tell him I had been trying for seven years to have a child.

My new husband was very busy and never around. He was gone so much, I started to wonder what he was doing most of the time. I still worked at the store and kept myself busy as well. I had been promoted to buyer, which meant I traveled a lot. We never saw each other. I sensed that something was wrong. I am not the smartest person, but I have instincts, and deep down, I knew. Besides, we weren't having sex, and that's a pretty strong indication of trouble in a marriage.

He never wanted sex when he came home. Sometimes he would meet me on the road, at a hotel, when I was traveling—in retrospect, I guess he was maintaining the charade that became our marriage, since he didn't want his fourth marriage to fail. We would kiss good night, and yet he wouldn't touch me. When I asked him why, he said he had back pain. I asked him how we were supposed to have kids, and he told me we'd just have to wait until his back got better. About five years passed, and he and I still hadn't conceived. Of course, I didn't have many opportunities to conceive, since we had infrequent, obligatory sex. I wanted a baby with a man who was going to be there for me. It meant more to me now then ever before. I suspected that my new husband was cheating, although I had no proof. Every time I asked him about it, he accused me of starting an argument.

I took a two-week buying trip abroad and felt so lonely I could have choked. My husband and I hadn't made love in months, and I was feeling rejected and depressed. My self-esteem was nonexistent. There was little doubt in my mind that my eight-year-old marriage was going down the tubes, and my biological clock was ticking like a time bomb.

I had to do something. One of the other buyers for the men's department at a tony New York store was there. He was handsome, and we started flirting. I noticed that he wore a beautiful, elegant white-gold wedding band studded with diamonds. One thing led to another, and the next thing I knew, we were sleeping together. He said that his wife had cheated on him twice, but he still wanted to stay in the marriage. He loved her and loved his family. His wife was pregnant, and I was secretly jealous. He said that sex with his wife was terrible—that she had done nothing but lie there for the past few years. He wanted passion, romance, and just some good old hot sex.

We slept together that first night, and since my husband couldn't give a shit about where I was or what I was doing, we stayed in the same room for the rest of the trip. We lived together for those two blissful weeks. I knew I couldn't get pregnant, so I saw no need for using protection. We had great sex every night. I guess I should have been worried about AIDS and herpes, but I figured since he was married, there was no reason for concern.

Going home was tough. We'd fallen in love and didn't want to leave each other. We promised to get together back in the States and keep in touch by phone. We even flew back together, and much to our surprise, when we walked off the plane almost arm in arm, his eight-months-pregnant wife was waiting for him. There I was, having spent the last fourteen years trying to get pregnant, and here was this pregnant woman, the wife of the man I'd spent two weeks screwing every night. I felt jealous, scared, and simply awful. I ran ahead of him. I had such tremendous conflict, I was nearly out of control: On the one hand, I was in love with this man, but he had cheated on his pregnant wife. I wanted to rip my skin off, I felt so shitty. What the hell was I doing with my fucked-up life?

I called my husband from my cell phone on the way home from the airport. I needed to talk, but I couldn't find him anywhere. I tried his office, the house, his cell phone. He was nowhere to be found.

When I got home, I was worn out and emotionally drained. I desperately needed to figure out my life. When my husband finally came home, I asked him what the hell was going on. He told me he'd had an affair because he wasn't feeling connected to me. He confessed, as though I didn't know, that not having sex with me over the years had nothing to do with his bad back. He said he loved me but needed someone who could make him feel more like a man.

I was miserable and in disbelief. I confessed my own affair. We cried, fought, and hit each other, and after hours of this turmoil, which went on all night long, we decide to give it another go. We made love, and he actually paid very close attention to every part of my body. I felt complete and in love with my husband again. For weeks and weeks, I thought of my lover and those two weeks in Europe, but I decided that I wanted to make my marriage work.

When my lover called, I was abrupt with him. Their new baby daughter had been born. His wife had complications, and she was still recovering. I could barely speak to him; I was completely involved in making my second marriage work.

I was always a skinny person, a size four, and I was suddenly putting on weight, which was quite noticeable on my small frame. I figured the weight gain was because I was falling in love with my husband again, and I didn't have time for the gym because all my free time was for us. About four months after I came back from Europe, I went for a regular checkup with my gynecologist. She did a pregnancy test, because upon examination, she said she'd felt something and needed to confirm her suspicion.

When I got home, my doctor called and said I was four months pregnant. I was shocked, stunned, and elated at once. I called my husband with the good news. He didn't seem as elated as I was, since he quickly calculated the dates and realized that during our reconciliation and our true-confession time, the baby could be my lover's. He wasn't going to be happy until the baby was born and we could do a paternity test. I called my ex-lover, who was not only stunned by the news but seemed a little happier than my husband. I told him how my husband had reacted, and he told me that he wished the baby I was carrying was ours.

When the baby was born, he looked just like my husband and me. I was certain that he was ours. My husband didn't feel the same way. He said the baby's coloring was markedly different from anyone in his family. We did the test and the baby was 99.9 percent not his. That was the end of my marriage.

After a few months, I called my lover to tell him that I had a beautiful baby boy (a poignant moment for my lover, since his other children were girls) and that my husband had moved out. I was so happy to have my baby that I didn't care who the daddy was.

I wondered if perhaps I hadn't been able to conceive before because it takes true love for that to happen. My lover came to see the baby. It was love at first sight. He promised me that he was going to be a good daddy. He explained that he couldn't leave his wife because she'd suffered some permanent complications after the second baby was born. He felt obligated to stay with her. But he wanted to be a part of our lives, too, something I felt was not only ridiculous but unnecessary. I wanted to raise my baby and be happy without all of the confusion. I loved him, but I knew I couldn't have him. He visits his son to this day.

I still yearn to be with my lover. My third husband is a fine man, but he is a good deal older than I am. He offers me companionship and stability, and I have come to realize that the most important thing in life is family, something I now have with my child and my husband. But as I said, I still yearn for what once was and never can be.

Mrs. T

Mrs. T is a stunning woman in her late fifties with the looks of a mature model. She lives in Sun Valley, Idaho. She is divorced after a twenty-four-year marriage that, to her regret, bore no children. Her ex-husband recently remarried. During our meeting, men stared as if wondering who she was: She exudes the aura of a celebrity. She is completely no-nonsense and was slightly amused by our questions. We talked for hours about men and sex and why she had cheated. She admitted that she used both her beauty and brains to make the business she shared with her ex-husband into more of a success. She was very matter-of-fact about her marriage. She is a woman who clearly requires attention, and at times during her marriage, she flirted with some of their business associates to get what they needed for the company. Then there was the time when the flirtation went too far.

The affair happened as my marriage was deteriorating. Sure, I knew the marriage was just about over, but we were still playing the game and doing what we had to do, even though it was just a charade. That's what people did thirty-five years ago. You got married and stayed married, period, right?

I had always been tempted by the idea of affairs, because men flirted with me all the time. Most of the men who flirted with me were my husband's friends. I suppose that's often how affairs happen.

It wasn't until the last five or six years of marriage that I was in it only for the money. We had built a business together, and I wasn't going to let all of my hard work go to waste. Our relationship had become mundane and perfunctory. Very much along the lines of "Hello, how are you?" When a woman loses the lust for her husband, she's faking everything. And toward the end, I was pretty damn good at faking orgasms as well as at being a wife. I had no illusions about the fact that it was the money that kept me with my husband.

There came a point, however, when I couldn't take it anymore and wanted the marriage to be over. I had sex with him just to avoid an argument. The sex became so bad that I would lie there and turn my head so I wouldn't have to look at him. Once I accepted that the marriage was ending, I had to figure out a crafty way to get a lot of the money.

I had married my husband when I was around thirty, and I was in love with him. He had a brain, and we could converse; I've always felt communication is intrinsic to a marriage. He had recently divorced and had very little money, but two days before our wedding, he asked me to sign a prenuptial agreement. I was filled with doubt after that—I wondered if he loved me less, didn't trust me, or was simply reacting to his divorce. Given the fact that he had no money, why was he asking me to sign a prenup? I was kind of reluctant to go ahead with the marriage. I also thought he was sneaky, asking me to sign the agreement two days before we got married. I asked myself why this hadn't come up before. Nevertheless, we got married as planned.

As soon as we got married, I felt I'd made the right decision and that he was the right guy. Our marriage wasn't just financially motivated in the beginning. It wasn't until we started our business, when we became extremely wealthy, that things changed.

One day I came home and he suggested that we watch porno movies. I couldn't figure out where that was coming from, and frankly, I was a bit offended. He said that if I wanted to please him, I would go along with him. I knew I wanted to please my husband, so I played along in the beginning. I was really thinking, What am I doing? Aren't I enough to satisfy his sexual appetite? Why do we have to watch a movie of people doing what we could be doing without the movie that makes everything seem lewd and disgusting? At first he wanted the movies on from time to time, but then it became all the time and always when we were having sex. In fact, he couldn't even get it up unless these movies were on. I wondered, Where is he learning this stuff? Who is giving him these ideas?

While the movies played, he wanted to make love for two hours, and I was ready to go to sleep. We had so many arguments over those porno movies. It became such a pain to have sex with him. Not to mention that I began thinking he couldn't really love me if he needed the porn as an incentive all the time. But when I got married, I got married for good, so I took it. I was just a pretty lady standing by her man.

One time when we were traveling in Europe with another couple, we were at lunch, and my husband asked the table what type of wine we'd like. I responded quite confidently, "I'm feeling like red today, since it's such a crisp day." He stopped, looked at me, looked at everyone else at the table, and said, "Who the hell is asking you?" I responded, "I thought you were asking everyone." After that incident, he didn't speak to me for three days. He ruined everyone's vacation. After that, he went on a drinking binge, something that wasn't unusual for him—he was a big drinker—but this time he went over the top.

Suddenly, I realized that I was there to fulfill his basic needs and nothing else. His behavior was going to ruin our empire. I had given up my identity, and between the porn and his verbal abuse and drinking, I wanted it back. That was the impetus for my affair.

I met the guy through one of my business contacts. It's a funny thing: I wasn't looking for an affair. It just happened, almost out of my conscious control. All of a sudden, I found myself having sex with this man. I can barely remember the circumstances. All I knew was that my husband wasn't coming home, something that wasn't unusual back then, even though we hadn't officially separated. We were still living together, but in name only. My lover and I were having sex in my house. I couldn't help myself. It felt good and I wanted more. I hadn't felt that way in years, not even when my husband and I first got married. My lover brought me back to life in a sense. We had sex in every room.

I wasn't brought up to cheat, yet I don't regret having the affair. I actually wish I could have enjoyed sex with my husband, but I just couldn't. When my husband came home the night my lover and I had slept together in the house, I just stared at him. I couldn't sleep with him, even though I felt I was supposed to. I just couldn't believe I had slept with another man and it had felt so good. I knew I couldn't sleep with my husband again. I had to get a divorce.

I stayed with my husband long enough to make certain I wouldn't lose out financially. Most women don't know how to set themselves up financially, and most men will try to take everything. That's why so many women become poverty-stricken after a divorce. That wasn't going to be me, that was for sure. I made out well, and my lifestyle hasn't changed much at all.

My husband has since remarried and is miserable. My lover and I have remained friends, and we see each other from time to time, but basically, I am happy, and happy being single. Sometimes I think I'd like to get into another relationship, but I would never marry again. I date, and I like hanging out with my friends. My bottom line is that I am independent: I can afford to support myself for life and will not end up a pauper.

Mrs. U

Mrs. U lives in southern New Jersey. In her forties, she has been happily married for fourteen years, and she and her husband have two children. In her day, she says, she was considered a stunner. Although she admits that she could probably afford to lose about fifteen pounds, she's comfortable, and guys often hit on her. She has brown skin, light green eyes, shoulder-length brown hair, and a beautiful smile. For fifteen years, Mrs. U and her husband have owned a restaurant together, and that's where she says she got herself into a bit of trouble one snowy night.

After my husband and I were married, we had children and moved to the suburbs. We ran our restaurant together, as we still do, each of us with well-defined duties. I am the "face," there every evening to greet the diners and the bar guests, and to make sure everyone enjoys themselves and has a pleasant time. My husband is more behind the scenes, running the day-to-day business. He orders supplies, keeps the books, works with the chef, plans the menus, and makes sure we have the best possible produce, meats, and fish.

Our arrangement has always worked well. It allows me the time to be a mommy, to hang with the kids all day, to bake cakes, to go to PTA meetings, and things like that, while my fabulous husband gets everything ready for the evening. Because I'm the personality of the restaurant and I have to be there when things start popping, usually at night, a lot of men hit on me. I still enjoy the attention.

When the kids were younger, my husband and I did the handoff at about six in the evening, and I stayed at the restaurant well into the night, sometimes until three or four in the morning. Although I enjoyed being with my young children all day, I loved being at the restaurant, and being the star at night.

It was a turn-on and a thrill. When I walked in, the lights were dim, and everybody stopped in their tracks to acknowledge me. At the same time, I felt our kids were well cared for, because they had me all day and their daddy at night to put them to bed and read them stories. He was so good with the kids, probably better than I was. I got to be their daytime nurturer, but he was the last face they saw before they went to sleep at night.

Benny had come to our restaurant once or twice a week from the time we opened. He became one of the regulars, so we would always make small talk. There was something attractive about him, although he wasn't my type.

I'd had a few drinks one evening and was feeling a little tipsy. I had to go in the back and make some change for a customer. I noticed that Benny was in the back of the restaurant, seemingly arguing on the phone with someone. He was getting loud, but the restaurant was so loud it didn't really matter. As I said, I thought Benny was kind of cute, but I was a very happily married woman. Nothing could make me want to cheat on my husband. Even though our sex life wasn't as sizzling as it had once been, I had so much fulfillment in my life. That night, however, as I drove home, I thought about Benny.

The next night the weather prediction was bad, so I planned to stay overnight on the couch in my office if I couldn't get home. By the time I got to the restaurant, there was already some snow accumulation, so I was resigned to settling in for the night. I went through my chores and had a quick glass of wine before the evening rush. The expected rush turned into a trickle of a few of my regular patrons, one of whom was Benny. He looked good, and since I'd had a few glasses of wine—well, maybe it was more like a bottle—I was feeling very relaxed.

It was a cold winter night, and I was in a strange mood. The place was quiet. I bought Benny a drink, and we sat and talked for most of the evening. We ended up having dinner together at the bar and just couldn't stop talking. As it became more apparent that he wanted to get closer, I reminded him that I was married, and cautioned him that I wasn't interested in playing around. After more wine and more time, the conversation became more intimate. He talked about sex and what pleased him. I enjoyed talking about sex with him, but I knew if we continued, something was going to happen. I felt that he was seducing me.

As we continued to talk and flirt, the bartenders and waiters wanted to know if they could go home or if I was going to keep the bar open for a while. I sent them home, telling them I would lock up. I told Benny that I was going to spend the night on the couch, and I said he should get ready to go. He said I shouldn't be alone in the storm and offered to sleep on the floor. I protested, but he said that he had to be back at work in a few hours and didn't want to risk the drive home and the possibility of getting stuck. He said he'd sleep in his car if I wouldn't let him sleep on the floor. Foolishly, I said okay.

We went downstairs, and I made a little makeshift bed for him on the floor. I slept on the couch without opening the convertible bed. I was very uneasy. I knew I wasn't doing the right thing, that I was putting myself in a compromised position.

Needless to say, he seduced me. He came over to me and whispered in my ear that he wanted to taste me. That sort of thing hadn't happened in my marriage for so long. I wanted to feel that wonderful sensation one more time. When Benny touched me, I thought I was going to melt.

The foreplay was even more enjoyable than the sex, and I savored every single second of it. My entire body felt electrified. It all felt just right at that moment. I made him leave at six in the morning. I didn't want to take a chance of anyone finding out. I called my husband as soon as Benny left, to tell him how lonely I was, and how much I missed him and the kids. I also said that I was coming home and wanted the next night off.

I know this sounds outrageous, but that night with Benny was the greatest, the most outstanding, maybe the best sex I've ever had. But I never want to do it again. I didn't feel guilty as much as a little embarrassed and duplicitous. Everyone thought I was happily married, and I was—so how would I explain my behavior if anyone found out?

I love my husband. My indiscretion that night is something no one will ever know about. I made Benny swear to never mention it to anyone, and I said if he did, he would be very sorry, although I didn't know how I would carry out the threat.

I went back to my wonderful life with my wonderful family, but I will never forget the night I had with that man. Although I am now saying I'd never do it again, I hope like hell I can keep that promise.

Would Like to Do That

Dreaming On

It didn't come as a surprise to discover that the women who had merely fantasized about infidelity felt more distraught and far guiltier than those who acted on their fantasies. They were more concerned about being found out for their thoughts than the others were for their actions. This group was more reluctant to talk; they needed more coaxing and assurance of anonymity. Until they came to trust us, they wouldn't give us their phone numbers, and when they did, they cautioned us gravely about when to call, and under no circumstances were we to leave a message on their machines.

In our opinion, the number of women out there with fantasies is nearly infinite. As a matter of fact, when we sent out our queries—either through bulk e-mails to friends, with a request to forward them to their friends, or when we made phone calls as we networked—we were astounded by how many women not only denied ever having had an affair but adamantly denied fantasizing. We got the distinct feeling that this group was so guilty for their thoughts that even admitting that once in a while they thought about another man might somehow "get them in trouble."

We grew up in a generation in which fantasy was deemed healthy. We fantasized as little girls about our wedding days, had crushes on boys, and wondered what it would be like if he called. For sure, as we've dished with our girlfriends over the years, there have been few who haven't entertained the notion of "what if " when it came to an old beau from high school or college—so why all the denial? Our guess is that admitting the fantasy teeters on the precipice of reality. Of this group, how many will eventually have affairs? Since we have neither crystal balls nor degrees in psychology, it's a tough question to answer, but going just on woman's intuition, our guess is that certainly half of them will fall into the Doing That category.

Although so many potential interviewees declined and denied within this category, there is no question that the women who agreed to be interviewed have only fantasized. But the fantasy, although it gets them through the times when life is all too mundane and unexciting, seems to be as tantalizing and forbidden as the real thing—for now.

The natural question is, why such guilt over nothing, as though the mind police were staking out their psyches. We can only presume that it's because fantasy has no ceiling. Their minds take them places where no one would ever know they dared to travel, and both the journey and the destination are somewhat frightening. Moreover, the fantasy is within their control. It can have the happy perfect ending. But fantasy appears to be both an emotional and intellectual betrayal. There is the additional element of their own sense of duality, as many lie awake beside their husband at night thinking about another man; that tortures them and leaves them feeling panicked at unrequited desires.

Ironically, there appears to be less rationalization and justification among these women. Fantasy is private. It has not become so much a part of their lifestyle, in the way that a physical affair has to be calculated and tailored and handled with discretion, as well as reasoned away. These women are honest with themselves about the betrayal they are contemplating, and they combat frustration and loneliness as they wonder if their dreams and hopes will remain only smoky images in the middle of lonely nights.

Once they had confessed their fantasies, they gave an outpouring of gratitude when we told them they were not alone. It made them feel, as so many said, "less crazy." Many of the women called back several times to offer more information, spilling more about their thoughts and needs, their words tumbling out of them now that they had a safe forum.

Said Mrs. W, "Sometimes I'll see a man, an artist like me, and I'll think how great it would be to be with someone who does what I do and shares this passion. I wonder what it would be like to have a physical relationship with that man. I think about it—and then the gallery closes or the party ends and I go home and I'm back to reality. I'll always wonder what it would be like and what I would do if I got out of this rut. Would it be spectacular or disastrous? The devil I know as opposed to the devil I don't know."

MRS. V

Mrs. V, forty-eight, is the mother of two children and lives in a suburb of St. Louis, Missouri. She is a graphic artist and has been married quite happily for fourteen years. But Mrs. V is not without her fantasy. He is the first love of her life, the boy she loved in high school. She speaks with him now and then, and she thinks back and wonders what if, but reality remains more appealing. Of fantasy, she says, "While life may not be the party we hoped for, while we're here, we might as well dance." The fantasy tides her over during the moments when the mundane is overwhelming.

R obert and I have known each other since the third grade. The first time I saw him, my mother was returning a book to the neighbors across the street, and he came to the door. That was the first time he registered. We ran into each other again at church functions, and as we got older, he started hanging around me at school. At sixteen, I was in one of those phases, those once-in-a-lifetime things, when three guys started liking me at the same time. That wasn't typical for me at all. I remember once when Robert was coming up the walk and I had a date with this other guy and I hid in the bathroom and begged my dad to tell Robert I wasn't home. My mother never would have lied for me, but my dad did. The summer before we started dating, Robert wasn't around, and to my astonishment, I started to miss him. I felt terrible because I had been so rude to him the year before. I mean, I walked down the hall at school with him, but that was really all. The next year my girlfriends told me that Robert wanted to ask me to home-coming. It took him a zillion tries to get up the nerve. We went to home-coming, and after that, we began to really date.

We had a nasty breakup, though, when we headed off to college. We got back together over Christmas, and in between, there were these intense peri-ods of letter-writing. He met a girl in his senior year, and we had another unpleasant breakup.

After he graduated, he started working for a newspaper in Chicago. He'd always wanted to be a reporter. I was in Boston at the time, and even though it was rather long-distance, we got back together again, saw each other a few times, and then broke up again. And then, believe it or not, I started working in Chicago! It was the first time since high school that we'd been in the same town.

We were working a block and a half away from each other. I can't re-member whether he knew I was working there. I would walk by his office at lunchtime, you know, trying to run into him. Finally, I decided that was crazy and just called him. We dated for a month, and he moved to another newspaper down in Florida, and I never heard from him. I wrote him a nasty letter, but he never got it. About a year later, a mutual friend of ours from high school told me that she'd heard he was getting married. Fortunately, that news came just days after I met Matt (my future husband, although I didn't know that at the time). It was a shock, but it wasn't as devastating as it could have been. Now, understand, I never slept with Robert. I was this re-ally straight shooter, you know? Robert was never an affair of anything more than the heart.

Our whole situation has always been so weird. You know, it was like you can run but you can't hide. To this day I'll meet people who know someone who knows someone who's an old friend of Robert's or mine from Cleveland and somehow they connect the two of us. And there are still the times when I'll be thinking about him and "our" song comes on the radio. I've always felt with him that it's like sliding doors.

Well, he got married, and I was still working in Chicago and dating my husband, but we weren't even close to marrying. I was in touch with people from all over the country. It had been five years since I'd talked to Robert. My phone rang, and he told me that his paper in Florida was sending him to cover a big event I was working on. He was married and had a child. He said he wanted to get together. At first I hesitated, but then he said that he wanted to explain why he'd acted the way he had five years before. I said that sounded really interesting, but could we have this discussion after I threw the huge event? So we planned to meet on the Friday night after the event. That meant I would have seen him in passing the day before and gotten my feet wet, and then we could have our heart-to-heart. The day before the event, I decided to walk uptown with my friend Jennie, even though it was way out of the way, and then take the El to an appointment I had. Well, I ran into none other than Robert, who was waiting for someone at a restaurant. It turned out that he was waiting in the wrong place. So there I was, fretting for years about running into him, and I was not where I was supposed to be, and he was not where *he* was supposed to be—and there we were. There was this street-person drug addict lurking around who grabbed Jennie and kissed her hand, and then he started handing out these little red paper hearts. It was almost Valentine's Day. And it was freezing and windy and just so bizarre. You know, if you had that in a book, the scene would be edited out as too corny and unbelievable.

Anyway, Robert and I got together that Friday, as planned. He came to my apartment to get me, and I read him a letter that I had written to him years before (I'd kept a copy of it) after one of our breakups. He made a phone call from the phone booth outside before we went to dinner, and I assumed he was calling his wife. I didn't really want to know. Even now she doesn't know that we're still in touch. My husband knows that I speak to Robert once in a while. After that evening I felt that the situation between us was finally resolved. I felt that we could finally turn the page and close the chapter. Robert kissed me good night, and I thought, Hmmm, now, this is fun. And I thought, So this is probably how affairs start. It was the first time that the notion of an affair had really slapped me in the face. I thought I understood how those things happened and why people had affairs, but I didn't. The next day I woke up and had a horrible headache and felt totally nauseated and thought, What if this? and What if that? and made myself nuts. Matt came to pick me up, and I said, "Just be careful with me today, because I've just had a rather emotional experience." Robert still has that kind of emotional impact on me.

We saw each other a year or so ago at our high school reunion back in Cleveland. It had been eighteen years. We did have a correspondence before the reunion—we started writing once the date was set, and we called to see if the other would be there. Since the reunion, we e-mail and stay in more regular touch. It's very much on the up-and-up, but it always gives me pause when I see his e-mail address pop up on my computer screen.

Anyway, we decided to meet one-on-one before the reunion. We met at the library. I got there first. I was waiting for him in this little parklike area with benches, and there was a guy coming toward me, and he was somewhat portly and had a bald spot. I thought maybe . . . but it wasn't Robert. When he arrived, Robert looked good. Really good.

We started talking, and it felt like yesterday. He kind of moved in a little closer to me on the bench as he talked to me. There was this air of familiarity, and an odd and exciting tension in the air. When we were at the reunion, he played it very close to the vest. When we were around our former friends, I was careful not to let on that I knew as much about Robert's life as I did.

It's always so easy to talk to him. Sometimes I feel like our relationship isn't over. One time he joked that when our spouses kicked, we'd get together. I know these types of things aren't the safest to say, but we go there sometimes; he goes there more than I. I don't know if he's happily married. I suppose he's as happy as anybody.

Sometimes I think back to a few weeks before my wedding, when Robert called. I thought he'd called because he'd seen my picture in the hometown paper, but as it turned out, he'd just called out of the blue. I told him that I was getting married in two weeks, and he was shocked. He said that tugged at his heart, and it was all I could do not to ask him why *he* had gotten married seven years before. So much for sliding doors. Thinking back to that moment is one of the thoughts I have late at night when the house is sleeping and I lie there awake, thinking.

One friend from home doesn't think it's a good idea that Robert and I communicate as much as we do. Another friend thinks it's okay that we're still in touch because we were so close. Without a doubt, there's a part of me that's still in love with him. He owns a piece of my heart—the first-love part of my heart—and why should I give that up? That's how I look at him.

I think the fantasy is probably better than the reality. I once talked to him about that, and I said I was certain he did all those annoying things that all men do. But I don't live with him, and if I did, maybe it would wreck the fantasy and the romantic notions. I think it's better in some ways that he's out there and not with me.

Sometimes I feel disloyal or unfaithful just *thinking* these things. Marriages, as you know, have peaks and valleys. You get along better sometimes than other times. My fantasy is sitting on a fishing boat with Robert and talking. Then life would be grand. That would be the place where I would be the most peaceful.

Matt has been pretty decent lately. He knows I saw Robert at the reunion, but I didn't tell him we met at the library. I have this sense that Matt has a thing for his old high school girlfriend. I don't think his connection is as romantic as mine, since he doesn't stay attached the way I do. Frankly, I don't want to know. We don't talk about it, and I don't want to talk about it. I think we both know that we have some connections to people from our pasts, but neither of us wants to go there with each other. Maybe it's that we don't want each other in those fantasies.

When I got home from the reunion, I told my daughter that I'd seen my old boyfriend, and she asked why Robert and I had never married. I told her that he wanted to get married too early and I wanted to have a life first. She asked me if he took me to prom, and then she asked if I was in love with him. I thought that was strange. Out of the mouths of babes.

I have an okay marriage. I used to think it was more decent until I saw Robert at the class reunion, and now I think I would never get married again if Matt and I didn't work out. I wish Matt didn't watch so much television. That really bugs me. He's not as much of a doer as I wish he would be, but then again, I'm so wired. I suppose if we were both like me, we'd drive each other totally crazy. He's not probing or analytical or emotional. Once he joked when he'd heard that Robert had called, and said, "Can't you two leave each other alone?" But he was truly just joking. He knows I wouldn't do anything. There's a trust.

I do think that Matt and I have drawn the line. It's sort of like "Whatever, I don't have to know everything you do." I think that people can have another facet of their lives that makes them more interesting, and telling about it might make the other person feel bad, especially when it's just a fantasy. One thing for sure—I would never want Matt to stay married to me if he thought there was someone who could make him happier. I wouldn't want an obligatory relationship.

I've thought about having an affair with Robert, but I know I could never do that while my kids are still at home. The idea becomes especially tempting when Matt and I hit one of those low points in our marriage. It becomes one of those things that I think I could do if I hit one of those lows after my kids are away, but now it's too risky and would be too tough on the kids. It's the same thing when I think about divorce: Matt and I love our kids so much that divorce is something we wouldn't even consider. I don't want to jeopardize my kids in any way. If I didn't have the kids, it would be a totally different deal. It's amazing how my kids hold me back from doing a lot of things!

Mostly, I wish I could have talked to Robert for much longer than we did that day at the library. I don't think he has the same communication with his wife. That day at the library, we both wore sunglasses, and yet I could feel him looking into my soul. He has often said to me that he feels I know him better than anyone else. We have a history together—a childhood together. We really know what the other is all about. I think if our spouses ran off with other people and we could be together, we would sustain that feeling of being soul mates. Sometimes I fantasize about that. One can only hope.

If a genie came out of a bottle and said I could go off for the weekend with Robert and there would be no repercussions, and that my husband and kids would never know and there would be no hurt and no pain for anyone, would I do it? Yes, but it would be really scary. What if I found out that he could make me happier? Keeping this at bay makes it easier and more palatable. There are so many things I don't know about Robert as the man he is now. And after the initial glow wears off, there are things you find out about someone that can make you nuts. I know those things about my husband because I live with him. Some of the things I know about Matt now, after living with him all these years, *do* drive me nuts. It's the eternal what if. But I think that fantasies like this one can help a marriage. I think if you take what you know about your fantasy and try to apply it to your marriage, then it can help. You know, like "I just said this really nice thing to this person I'm not married to—maybe I should say something like that to my husband." I may not get that soulful penetrating look. I mean, I could say it to my husband, and he would look at me like I had two heads, and then he'd click the remote control. It's a tough call. I think about this fantasy man and believe I would ruin the fantasy if I married him. I'm such a control freak, and yet with him, I feel out of control. But it's a rush, without a doubt. It's forbidden. And we're not even doing anything. This isn't about sex. And yet I think this is more romantic, and I still feel like I'm betraying my husband because I've let someone else into my heart.

But being married is more than romance. And having an affair is an escape from the drudgery of life. Marriage is sometimes all too real. Sometimes it feels like I get exhausted with life. The fantasy is just fun. The truth is, I would never have an affair because it would wreck the stability of my life and all the good things in my life, and it would wreck my husband. Sometimes life is so overwhelming. The fantasy takes me back to a simpler, gentler, easier time. But fantasy has to remain just that, or it becomes another reality, and then you have to find another way to escape in your head.

I don't want to give up my marriage or my life. I also want to keep my fantasy. The fantasy makes the reality of my life a whole lot easier.

MRS. W

&⁊

Mrs. W is a fifty-year-old mother of three children, two boys and a
girl. She has been married for twenty-two years and lives in a suburb
of Philadelphia. Although she presents herself as sexually disinterested
and even uptight to her husband, and the quintessential mom to her
kids, she has a secret inner life that's filled with lust and longing. She
craves romance and passion. She watches romantic movies and allows
her mind to wander to the point of desperation. Her marriage is not
what she wants. It's not what she ever wanted. A long time ago, before
she was married, a boy hurt her so badly that the wound never even
formed a scar. She thinks about him still—not so much because she
wants that romance back but because she wishes she hadn't allowed
herself to be so wounded. She now wishes that she had waited and let
the wound heal before she rushed into a marriage that didn't feel right
from the start. The problem was, she thought she'd never love again.
Now the problem is, she wants to love again, but with whom? Mrs. W
is a painter. Her husband is a statistician. They are worlds apart.

I dated a fair amount before I got married. And it was not great dating. I
met my husband in college. He was working at the university, and I was
getting a graduate degree. He's a year younger than I am. I suppose that I was
in love with him when I married him but not in an infatuation kind of way.

What I mean is, there were no butterflies in my stomach, as I'd had with boys, one in particular, when I was a really young girl. I married him because I liked him. It seemed comfortable with him. It was the right time, and I respected him. He's a very smart man. So, in all those capacities, I can say that I loved him. My feet were on the ground, though. I very much wanted to have children, and that was a tremendous incentive. It was that old now-or-never.

I had a relationship prior to marrying in which I was terribly hurt. That was the relationship that made me feel the butterflies. The one where my feet weren't on the ground. It lasted a few years, and I was nineteen when we broke up. It sounds so young, but it didn't feel that way at the time and it doesn't feel that way even when I think about it now. After we broke up, I wasted a few more years pining over him and hit rock bottom. It took a long time for me to recover. I don't really know exactly why it ended. We were young, and to me it seemed like he was the man I would marry. But one day he said he couldn't make the commitment. Then he turned around and started seeing someone else and married her a year later. Who knows? I guess he just decided to take another path and left me in the dust, and instead of taking it well, I cried and ran after him until I just couldn't run after him anymore. It shocked me when he ended the relationship, but I should have just walked away with my head held high. Instead, I groveled and kept crawling back to his bed. It makes me sick now to think about how I belittled myself, but I was only nineteen, and I guess that's what we did back then when we were in love.

Even when I met my husband, I thought about that other boy. I wondered where he was and what he looked like. I still think about him. I know he's in the Midwest somewhere. To be perfectly honest, when I married my husband, I had a sense that I would never feel the way I had felt with that other boy, and I tried to accept it. I think my husband must have really loved me, though, when we got married. I'm a difficult person to get along with. My personality is much stronger than my husband's. I also think he was more attracted to me than I was to him.

My husband is very left-brained and very black-and-white. His whole makeup and upbringing are very different from mine. He's rigid and conservative and reserved. To me, he represented stability. At first I was certain he would hurt me as soon as we became physically involved. I thought right afterward, Well, that's it—now I'll probably never see him again. When he came back, it was such a shock. Once I realized he was coming back and that he truly cared for me, then the trust became established. I felt he wasn't out to hurt me and he would really stick around. That was a huge incentive. I'm not sure if "incentive" is the right word; perhaps it was more that it felt like the relationship could work and therefore I could proceed.

I felt happy on my wedding day. It felt like it was time, and my parents were happy and relieved to see me settled. We didn't have much of a honeymoon. We just went off to the beach for the weekend. We had jobs and responsibilities, and we couldn't take much time. I was okay with that, though. I'm somewhat of a homebody, so I wasn't eager to be away. To a large extent, what I had anticipated with my previous relationship was not what I was having. I wasn't the same person anymore. I had become rather hardened. Since that boy broke my heart, none of my subsequent relationships had made me feel truly happy and fulfilled. Part of it was that I knew I would never be in love the way I had been before, and another part was because I was just so bitter. I really hated men. Before I met my husband, when I was in my last years of college, I had a blind date once and fought with him. I had such a belligerent attitude. I was so angry. I carried that bitterness around with me for a long time.

So we've been married for twenty-two years, and I have been faithful to my husband. I'm faithful because if I wasn't, I would feel too guilty. My husband is a little insecure about me. When we first started dating, I was dating some other men as well, and he couldn't believe that I could date him and not give up these other relationships. He couldn't believe, even at the early dating stage, that I wasn't being exclusive with him. He still gets insecure when I do anything independent. If I go out to dinner with a male colleague, he gives me a funny look, like why am I doing that? He has no reason to feel that way. I've never given him any reason to feel insecure about the trust he can have in me. But I have lost a lot of weight, and maybe that makes him feel insecure, because I look a lot better than I did.

Maybe his insecurity also stems from a sense that I was never as in love with him as he was with me. It's also a sexual thing. I've never had a particularly active sex life with him. I would say that it was probably always just average. I knew it was something that was important to him, but it was easier for me to be persuaded to have sex before I had the kids. At this point in my life, it's hit an all-time low. It's because I don't want to have sex with him, not because he doesn't want to have sex with me. He's angry with me all the time because of that. Right now we haven't had sex in about six weeks.

I guess the reasons I haven't wanted to have sex with him are many. I was never particularly attracted to him, and I think about that boy who hurt me. I've never been attracted to a man like that since him. It's kind of a tall order to be that attracted to somebody. I've thought about if I'd waited longer to get married, if I had waited for the right man, maybe I wouldn't feel like this. Maybe I would have gotten over that boy if I'd married someone who really swept me off my feet. Maybe I didn't give myself a chance to heal. I wonder that a lot, especially lately. And I also wonder if I left my husband and were single again, whether I still have a chance to have that. It's something I would like to have with someone.

Recently, it hit me that you don't go through this life twice, and I wonder if that other relationship was that once-in-a-lifetime and I'll just never have it again, or maybe it's still out there. It's such finality to think that this is it. I'm locked in this marriage, and though I do love my husband on many levels, it's not in the way that I should or the way I would like to love someone. When I think that I will never have another chance at love again, it makes me feel old and very sad.

Even though I don't believe it will ever be possible, the longing is still there. I know also that I would be way too fearful to let go of what I have to seek it out and take the risk. There's that little part of me, though, that taunts me and says, "But imagine how wonderful it would be to feel that again. Give yourself a chance." Another voice tells me I'm mad to even think this way.

If I let the longing go and fantasize, I picture a walk on the beach, a quiet passion, a little bit of a torrid type of affair, conversation, comfort, and a consistent steady relationship, all of the above. All those thoughts belong to a side of me. The walk on the beach belongs to my independence. When I want to be touched, I want to be touched. When I want to be alone, I'll be alone. But I always would have and want the option of companionship. The torrid part is the part when I go to the movies and I see people who are making love on the screen and I think, Ooh, would I love to have that. I would want a steady relationship because I'm getting up there. I am a solitary person, but I don't want to be alone the rest of my life.

Things are going to change as my life goes on. I don't look like I did when I was thirty, and that's going to go even more. I want someone who's going to love me no matter how I look. One day I'm going to lose my mother, and I'm very close to her, and I want someone beside me. I know that my husband is not capable of giving me the emotional and physical comfort that I will need when I lose my mother, and this is very unfortunate. I think about this all the time. I think, God forbid anything should ever happen to our children, we would be the couple who would divorce.

There's a stability in my marriage that I have created by staying with him and having children and making a home, but I haven't allowed myself to lean on him emotionally, physically, or sexually. I have been very remote. I give myself 80 percent of the responsibility for the problems in my marriage. I'm tired. I throw a lot of myself into the kids and I guess only somewhat of myself into the marriage. It's all caught up to me lately. I want a piece of life back. I want to hone my skills. I feel a restlessness setting in that wasn't there before. If I let my husband in emotionally, then I am obligated to him sexually. I feel that if I even show him a tender touch, it will be taken as a sexual innuendo, and then I will be obligated. If I allow him to even hug me, then I'm as good as gone. That's a problem. If it could just stop at the hug, that would be good enough for me. I'm a tactile person but not in that respect. This is where my cat comes into the picture. He's my preferred companion. He's around when I want him to be, and he likes to be stroked, but he doesn't expect anything and his needs are simple. The cat doesn't make me feel guilty or inadequate.

When I have sex with my husband, it doesn't come naturally to me. I really have to work at it. And he loves sex. He's not unskilled, and he's gentle. He's a very touchy-feely guy—much more so than the average guy. He can stroke for hours. He would be very romantic if I allowed him to be. He's a "I want to please a woman" kind of guy, but I just don't want that from him. I'm not physically attracted to him. I don't know what I was expecting. Maybe I was expecting that this was the end of the road when I married him—that I'd have my children and that would be that. I didn't anticipate this stage of my life where I am suddenly having the same yearning that I had at twenty and twenty-five. I really think the whole thing is unfair to my husband. He's not an unreasonable person. Even if I said to him today, "I promise you that every two weeks we'll be together," he would be more than happy to pencil it into his calendar. He would be a different person. He'd be cheerful. He's been very sullen. It's obvious to both of us every day that the problem is there, looming over us—and the problem is me.

We haven't gone to therapy because he doesn't believe in therapy. I have gone for myself, but not specifically for my marriage. Basically, I just try to get through the days with my kids. The kids are my biggest challenge, and that's another issue for me. The amount of energy it takes for me—the emotional energy it has taken to get my kids to this point—has exhausted me. I suppose if I were in the kind of marriage I wanted to be in, I would find solace at the end of the day. But that would have to be with someone I felt was stronger. I married him because I thought he was safe, but he's not. I'm the stronger one. I wear the pants in this family. I'm the disciplinarian. I'm the hard-ass with the kids, and I don't like this role. It evolved this way because he doesn't handle things and uses "I'm not here, I'm working" as the excuse for not getting involved. I deal with all the hard stuff when it comes to the kids, and I think that's partially why I am so tired and closed up. At the end of the day, I want peace and quiet, but it would also be nice to do something stimulating from a perfectly sexual standpoint. Not a one-night stand. But just to have some sort of fire going with someone.

Although I don't necessarily support it, I think there's a reason why married women have affairs. If I had an affair and my husband found out, he would never forgive me. I wonder how some women manage to take that risk. I guess you have to work very hard at not getting caught. I question my lack of lust for my husband. He's successful and he's brilliant. Do I really want to embark on an affair and risk throwing it all away?

If I had some guarantee that everything would be amicable and we would both still walk our daughter down the aisle one day, I think I'd pick up and leave and just be by myself or maybe with someone else who gave me what I needed and what I wanted and who let me be independent. Someone who wasn't sitting there and brooding, waiting for me to come home if I was out for the evening or away for the day. Maybe I'd try having a mature relationship with someone, but it would have to be on my terms, and it would not be a marriage. I mean, how could you not want something like that? Sometimes I think the whole companion-versus-husband thing is much more appealing. I love the movie *Same Time, Next Year*—now, that's a fantasy. I could never do that, though. I come from a very guilt-ridden family. They're professionals when it comes to guilt, and they've taught me well.

I suppose it's also hard for me to justify having an affair because I blame myself for what's wrong in my marriage. My husband desires *me*. I don't desire *him*. There's a part of me that longs to have a really good relationship, a relationship outside my marriage, but I'm afraid that I wouldn't be able to live with myself. If my husband were emotionally abusive or if he was withholding from me, then maybe I could justify it, but then I would just walk out and start over with no problems, no guilt, no strings. I know my husband would never have an affair. I would be floored if he did. I'd be upset probably more because I would think I was supposed to be upset, but once it hit home, it would be a sobering thing for me. I wonder if it would make him more appealing. Probably not. That unattainable thing is always appealing when you're courting, but I don't think it would hold now. A part of me would be able to understand and justify if he had an affair because I have been withholding. And I would probably forgive him. I don't know whether it would change my life extensively. Although I might think, Wait a minute—if he can do it, then why am I so worried about having an affair? But then I'd wonder why we were even married. I suppose that for me, fidelity is a little string that holds everything together.

There have been periods of time over the course of my marriage when I felt there was the possibility that there was something igniting me when it came to my husband, but I think that was in the beginning, before we were married. The flame went out because it wasn't the same as when I was nineteen, and maybe it wasn't fair to expect that it would be or could be. Since then, it's been more like kindling than a flame.

I have such a hard time watching romantic and passionate movies with my husband. I'll watch them by myself. I feel self-conscious and almost embarrassed watching them with him, especially when there's sexuality on the screen. I suspect he's thinking either that it could be stimulating to us (which I need like a hole in the head) or maybe it makes him angry because we don't have a relationship like that. I think if he knew that I thought about sex and that I have longings, he would think that the resolution was so simple—let's just have more sex. He would say, "So, well, let's just do it—let's fulfill it."

He wouldn't understand the other things that are attached to it for me. He doesn't know why I am so repressed, and he doesn't care. He doesn't care what's going on in my head because he feels so rejected. We're way past that. And this makes me feel guilty because I'm not really repressed—I'm just repressed when it comes to him. Not only would it shock him to know about that side of me, he would be offended and hurt. And I don't want to hurt him. There's a part of me that used to love him. Now I'm just numb. There's a mighty tall wall between us.

If he walked out on me, I might feel relieved, but I'd also feel scared. If it actually happened and I found myself alone, I'm not sure I would like it very much. But again, it would be a balance of relief and fear. I'd like to think I might have a second chance at love, but that voice comes into my head, telling me it won't happen. I have a divorced friend who's very attractive, and she is so lonely. She wants it to happen and it hasn't. I know better than to think I would be able to slide one out the door and then another one in the door. I don't think I'm that sexy or appealing.

What kind of man would I want at this point in my life? I would like to be with someone who has a strong character, who's sensitive and independent, someone who appreciates the arts and isn't so black-and-white. Someone more spontaneous. And I don't mean sexually spontaneous—I mean someone who would show his feelings more. I'd like him to be more of a man. My husband doesn't deal with things. His recalcitrance, the stuff that I once thought made him safe, has taken on a life of its own. In that respect, he's like a needy child, and that's a real turnoff. I don't want to feel that a person is weaker or needier than I am. I don't want to be Mommy to someone who's supposed to be my lover, my husband. I don't want someone who's always going to question how I can possibly be happy if I'm away for a few days or out for the evening and not understand that I don't need to always be with him to be happy. When I'm around my husband, I feel like I can't breathe. I need to breathe.

Sometimes I'll see a man, an artist like me, and I'll think how great it would be to be with someone who does what I do and shares this passion. I wonder what it would be like to have a physical relationship with that man. I think about it—and then the gallery closes or the party ends and I go home and I'm back to reality. And then I think, I've looked at that other person, sitting there with his persona and his canvas, and maybe he's just a real jerk when you take off the veneer. So I go home to security and to the letdown. But I always wonder what it would be like and what I would do if I got out of this rut. Would it be spectacular or disastrous? The devil I know as opposed to the devil I don't know. I don't talk about this kind of thing to anyone, not even to my therapist, whom I have known for years. When I'm in session, I never get past the "I feel guilty because I don't have sex with my husband." My girlfriends often say that at this stage in life, they don't feel like having sex with their husband, or anyone else for that matter, but I don't get into that with them because it's way too personal. Funny, I wonder if any of them ever had an affair. I don't think so, but who knows what we keep and don't share.

If you get pushed to the point where you have to start over again with someone else, what are the odds that you're going to find that "click"? It seems so remote. There has to be another person out there who feels this longing. Think about the odds of finding someone who's the same age or a little older and is in the same place. Seems like it would be next to impossible, and yet I would be willing to bet that you'd go to your grave with that longing. That's another part that keeps us glued back to where we are. It's got to be a one-in-a-million shot that you meet someone and remarry and are madly in love. My old friend has remarried and is happy, and I'm glad he found happiness. And you know what? He probably wouldn't be the person I'm looking for now anyway.

Mrs. X

Mrs. X is a fifty-year-old artist living in a suburb of New York City. A Manhattan girl born and bred, she moved to the suburbs when her third child was two years old, roughly eighteen years ago. That was the beginning of a loneliness that set in deeply and never let go. Living in the suburbs was vastly different from the city. Her Wall Street husband came home late at night, long after the kids were sleeping and when she was quite spent from the day. But more, he had a life in the city that she no longer had, and she wasn't privy to it. He went to business dinners and firm parties without her, saying that it wasn't important and was too much of a bother for her to get a sitter and trek to the city. Invisible lines were drawn between the once happily married urban couple: In the city, there was togetherness; in the suburbs, she felt her husband merely came home to sleep. About two years after the move, they had another child, and when she went off to college last year, Mrs. X's husband moved out and back to Manhattan. The marriage was on the proverbial rocks, but it was clear to Mrs. X that her husband had been itching to leave for over a decade. She stayed behind in the suburbs, the place that had become home for both her and her children. Although she was never unfaithful to her husband, there were nights she lay awake fantasizing about another kind of life with a different sort of man. She thinks back and wonders about all the years she might have wasted by only dreaming.

S ince I was a little girl, all I ever wanted was the knight in shining armor. That was who I dreamed about. I often lay awake at night picturing my own fairy tale, envisioning the prince who might rescue me with promises of a happily-ever-after.

When my husband announced that we were moving to the suburbs, I had a knee-jerk sense of claustrophobia. I knew, despite arguments that the city was only a forty-minute train ride away and the same by car when not the rush hour, that my urban days were aborted. As much as I balked, because I was a city girl through and through, I figured I could make the best of things. I took a ramshackle house and made it into a country cottage. I did so many of the fix-it things myself, even though in the past, whenever I'd ever wanted anything done, I'd called the super. And I loved doing it. I learned to love the backyard instead of the avenues. I stopped sneezing after a while when the lawn was mowed. I wasn't working at the time, but that would have happened in the city as well—I'm an artist, and there was no way I was going to pay someone to raise my children so I could work and make less than the nanny. I figured when the kids were well ensconced in school, I'd try my hand at my art again. And I did. I've even had a few galleries show my work in the last decade—something I don't think my husband ever thought would come to fruition.

Despite making the best of it, my loneliness set in with immediacy once we made the move. I had pictured our life the way summers had been in my childhood, when my family and I rented houses at the seashore. My father came out on Thursday night and stayed through Monday night. On Thursday night, my mom piled all of us (we were four kids as well) into the station wagon. We were all freshly bathed, fed, and in pajamas, and we went to pick up Daddy at the train. Just like in all those fifties sitcoms, our father stepped off the train, scooped all of us up one by one, planted kisses on our cheeks, and pulled some sort of treat from his pocket—anything from a shiny new quarter to a candy bar. And then he slipped his arm around our mother's waist as we kids ran ahead to the car. It was idyllic.

Train-station nostalgia was preempted immediately, because my husband bought a second car. The end-of-the-day interlude where I would pile the kids into the station wagon and meet Dad at the train never happened. He opted to fight the traffic in lieu of riding home in the bar car. I'd hoped he'd take the 6:07 the way my dad did, and have just the faintest scent of Scotch on his breath and a relaxed air about him that said the day was done. Instead, he drove up the driveway with the radio blaring like a teenager, and he came up the steps grumbling and aggravated. He'd pour a beer and ask when the kids had gone to sleep. He rarely saw them during the week. By the time he got home, it was usually about two hours past their seven-thirty bedtime. I'd give him dinner and pick at my food, since by that time I'd had enough bread crusts cut off of peanut-butter-and-jelly sandwiches to fill me up. I always sat with him—had a glass of wine and tried to talk to him about my day and his day—but by then there was little room left for me. For sure, there was no room left for us.

Sometimes I'd lie in bed at night and wonder about old boyfriends. Most of them were married. I'd kept in touch with three or four of them and knew most of their wives. Of course, you never really know the truth about anyone's marriage unless you live it, but at least the image presented by my old beaus seemed a lot better than mine. Some of the old boyfriends still lived in Manhattan and had country homes on lakes and near the beach. Others had moved out to the suburbs as well, but their bent seemed different from my husband's. They were often doing projects on the weekend—building a deck, painting, making repairs around the house, spending time with the kids. I remember our first Halloween in the suburbs, before my fourth child was born. The kids were six, four, and two and a half, and I went trick-or-treating with them alone in the neighborhood. I saw our neighbors, husbands and wives, walking hand in hand while the kids raced ahead with flashlights, their voices piercing the night. I felt it somehow augured what my life in the suburbs would be.

That was when the fantasies began. They were amorphous, more often than not about a faceless man I didn't know and hadn't seen, but someone I pictured in my mind's eye—that prince I'd dreamed about as a child. Then there was one who was real and concrete: the contractor who worked on our first house, overseeing the installation of new kitchen cabinets, windows, and wood floors. While my neighbors complained as they moved into their new homes that their contractors never showed up, John was there constantly. Then he began to come around after the job was done. He'd always say that he happened to be in the neighborhood and wanted to check on everything and say hello. He was my age, also married with small children. At first I was naive, thinking that maybe he was just being friendly. I was so caught up with babies and a new home and finding my way around what felt like a foreign country that it never occurred to me he was interested. After a few months, I became interested, primarily because he paid attention to me and my husband didn't. I thought about John a great deal and looked forward to his visits. But I was still determined to make a go of my marriage. On some level, I felt guilty for my thoughts. On another level, I felt excited and grateful, and as corny as it sounds, I felt like a woman and not just a suburban mother.

A few days before Christmas, John came by one evening around seven-thirty with a bottle of Rémy. He said it was for us—my husband and me—a thank-you for the job and to wish us a Merry Christmas. Of course, my husband wasn't home yet, and looking back, I wonder if John knew that, since we'd chatted enough for him to know the schedule. The children were sleeping. We opened the bottle right then and there, at my insistence that we have a toast. I was feeling a little brazen, I guess. As we sat at the dining table, with the snow falling, maybe something would have happened, just a kiss perhaps, if that wasn't the one night that my husband came home early. The strange thing is, he didn't even blink or show an iota of jealousy. He got a glass, pulled up a chair, and joined us. I had the distinct feeling that I was no longer a sexual creature to my husband. I felt undesirable, and I questioned my own fantasies about John, thinking that he probably viewed me as a lonely housewife and a way to kill time.

That was the end of John. He stopped coming by. I suppose my husband's presence put him off. But there was a string of men who were flirtations and fantasies. The men we suburban wives meet are not wearing suits. They're armed with tools and fix everything that our husbands promise to repair and either forget about or are incapable of doing. They become our heroes of sorts, and if they're cute and flirtatious (and most of them are), we lonely wives become easy prey and victims of fantasy. I was never duped to the point where I felt special or outstanding when it came to these men. So although I fantasized, it didn't substitute for the fairy tale.

I have always known, from a very young age, where fantasies and reality separate. When I was twenty-two, I was married to another man, and I was way too young to be married. After the first two years, I began to feel desperate, not ready for the attachment and homesick. I was doing a stint as a courtroom artist for a murder trial. The trial went for weeks on end. Once the jury began deliberations (which took another week), a bunch of us went out for dinner every night as we waited for the verdict. There was a young man who took a liking to me. He, too, was married. A good-looking, sexy, bright guy, he had a sexy job as well, as the crime reporter for a well-known newspaper. Our conversation at dinner became more intimate as time wore on. He was unhappily married, too, or so he said. One night he asked me to come back to his hotel room. I looked him right in the eye and said, "No. In six months, your eyes will be as empty as my husband's. This isn't what I want." I never saw him again after that night, except in the crowd when the guilty verdict came in.

That story became my mantra over the years. Having an affair is like taking a painkiller: It's not that the pain is gone; you just don't care that it's there anymore. Fantasies are better. They take us away for a while. And I have this feeling that once the fantasy is indulged, it's not as much fun. Then it becomes just another entangled relationship.

Infidelity is not a moral issue for me. It's not laced with biblical codes and legalities. It's more that I feel it never would have solved anything. I wanted to be married. I wanted to make love to my husband. I wanted a life with my husband. Fantasy often quelled my thirst. The problem with fantasizing was that I wanted those scenarios with my husband. The fantasies tortured me, mainly because when they started to form in my head, my husband always made his appearance.

Did I waste the best years of my life not indulging my fantasies, my libido, my romantic notions? Lately, I'm not certain. Now that my husband is gone, I question all those late nights when he was "working" in the city. I wonder if I wasn't naive and too forgiving. Sometimes I think about all the years when no one touched me, and I wonder if it's too late now. The one thing I am certain about is that during all those empty years, at least I was true to myself.

MRS. Y

Mrs. Y is a psychiatrist in Marin County, California. She's forty-five and has been married to a hospital administrator for sixteen years. They have two children, ages thirteen and eight. The oldest child, a girl, has learning disabilities that affect every aspect of her day-to-day life. Mrs. Y has two dueling fantasies: There is an older man who is the object of her thoughts as she lies awake at night or daydreams. The other fantasy is that perhaps one day she will fall in love with her husband—something she hasn't yet done. Then there is a third fantasy, the one that drives the other two in many ways: that one day her daughter will lead a normal and productive life.

When I married Ed, I was a completely different person. There's no question in my mind that he was a good fit for who I was. I was in a different place, and I was a very different person. Many of Ed's attributes, which he still has, really complemented and supplemented me. I admired him; he was grounded and stable.

However, I went into the marriage blind. My experiences with men and relationships prior to marrying Ed were limited. I had little if anything in terms of comparison, but I put on my blinders to shield what I didn't want to see. Ed tends to be a passive personality, something that is difficult for me to contend with because I'm a real go-getter. In the beginning, I often felt like I had to boost him up; I also felt that I had to come down, because I was extremely assertive. I had to learn to quiet myself, and I had a hard time settling down.

As the years have gone by, I've matured and become more sophisticated, and much of my evolution is due to my husband, who has always been patient and thoughtful. He gave me self-confidence, and he remains a calming influence. I married Ed four years after I met him. The problem is, I wasn't in love with him. I suppose I married him because I was tired of being alone, even though I was only twenty-five. My background was complicated, and at the point when I married Ed, I wasn't holding up that well anymore. My depressed mother had left my avoidant father after twenty years of marriage, and left me at eighteen to care for my twelve-year-old brother. I don't know that I would have been able to fall in love with anyone when I met Ed. A self-protective quality enveloped me, not to mention that being a surrogate mother at eighteen left little room for me, since I was so busy worrying about everyone else. But I liked Ed very much, and I still do. I did have a passion for him sexually, and I still do.

Now I think I can fall in love, and that's where my fantasies take me. You see, to allow yourself to be in love, you have to also allow yourself to be vulnerable. It was easier to marry someone I didn't love, because if he cheated on me, stopped loving me, or left me, it wouldn't have hurt that much. It was emotionally safe.

The object of my fantasies is also a psychiatrist. My fantasies about him are all over the place. He's divorced, and I'm guessing he's close to sixty. I've known him for ten years, and I've had fantasies about him on and off. Sometimes the fantasy is more intensified when other things around me are feeling out of control. He offers a feeling of safety to me, a sense of the father figure. I like the way he looks at the world, the way he can cut through different layers with immediacy and confidence, and his ability to articulate with an incredible eloquence and vocabulary that makes him extremely sexy to me.

The strange thing is, Ed is also articulate and eloquent, but he's not particularly visceral. I think the psychiatrist's attitude and personality are the sort of thing I always looked for in my relationship with my father. Again, that element of safety. Somehow my psychiatrist tells me that everything is going to be okay.

There is a part of me now, a huge part, that feels comfortable with vulnerability. Up until a few years ago, I didn't have that. My daughter, my special-needs child, was the one who unwittingly rescued me. Her challenges have forced me to rework my psyche. She has enlightened me. It's been a powerful epiphany: I can be vulnerable and no longer frightened of who I am. I have finally come to realize that I can be strong and assertive but also fall apart a little and still survive. My heart might be punctured, but it's not shattered. For me to have this fantasy about the psychiatrist is evidence of a new emotional plateau, because even this limited fantasy leaves me open and vulnerable.

I don't think that the psychiatrist reciprocates my feelings. I've never let on to him that I feel the way I do. When I fantasize about him, my thoughts are both sexual and emotional. He's very heady, like me. We're in the same profession and work with the same types of children and adults. When I speak with him, I feel very pulled up and out. It's hard to say whether I envision an extramarital affair, or being with him in a marriage or an ongoing relationship. More often, I think about having the whole package, and yet the fantasy is rather amorphous. There's an energy I feel emanating from him. There's an intellectuality about him that sweeps me off my feet.

My husband and I have never been in counseling, and yet I think we have a mutual understanding. Maybe we're not as sexually active as other couples, but we're certainly not inactive, and he's always turned me on. We'll go through periods when we have sex the typical once a week, and then when we're on vacation, we're more active. Undoubtedly, it's helpful when the kids aren't around and we're more relaxed. Lately, our sex life hasn't been great, but we've had a lot on our plates with the kids and ailing parents.

I've thought about whether there is anything my husband could do or not do to fill the desire that makes me indulge my daydreams about the psychiatrist. I don't think there is. There's a tremendous amount of affection between us, which is something that still doesn't preclude my fantasy. The difficulties and impasses in our marriage are personality issues, a brain chemistry that's missing between us. He's not emotionally charged enough for me. Ed gives me good responses, for example, when I am talking to him about our daughter. His instincts are good. His heart is in the right place. But there is a part of me that gets frustrated, and I think that goes right to the heart of the female issue of wanting to be rescued—in my case, from this ongoing crisis that we have with our child.

I don't feel the energy from my husband that I feel when I am with the other man. For instance, when I talk to the psychiatrist about my child, I feel that he totally gets how I feel. My husband also gets the depth of my feelings, and I think his are the same. The difference is, I'll put my feelings out there, and Ed can't. He hits an emotional wall, and I sense it. Perhaps in this respect, he keeps himself in check because he doesn't want to be vulnerable.

It's not about sex or money. If I had to boil it down to one thing where he fails me as a husband, I couldn't. You see, it's really what I didn't do. I wasn't in love with him.

I feel terribly guilty when I entertain thoughts of having an affair with this other man. First of all, I would be betraying my husband, and second, it would be a betrayal of who I am and my own values. This is not to put a judgment on extramarital affairs. It's just not something that I ultimately want for myself. I would view an extramarital affair, for myself, as a failure in some respects.

Generally, I think that extramarital affairs are confusing and potentially dangerous. This isn't to say that I would never have an affair. I've learned that we never know what cards we're going to be dealt, so I never say never. But I would be terrified that if I were to be found out, it would break up my marriage. In my practice, I've seen that happen too many times. My husband would never forgive me. The thoughts comfort me. They're enough to get me through the hard times. Then I put on the brakes.

I absolutely think that the psychiatrist is more gratifying as a fantasy than if he evolved into a reality. I am too old for illusions: Sometimes I can be talking with him, and he'll say something that I find annoying, and it serves as a reality check. Just a couple of months ago, I was disappointed in something he said, and although I didn't say anything, I noticed that for weeks, I didn't have fantasies. A part of me was disgusted with him, even a little angry—all over a statement he made that I found offensive and disagreed with. Not to mention what if he turned out to be a lousy lover? Sex can sometimes leave you feeling empty. Fantasy can fill you up a lot more.

When I allow myself to muse and take myself into the fantasy, it fills a void for me. I picture myself being madly in love with this other man.

Now here's the kicker: Sometimes I think about when our children are older, and Ed and I can be alone; I do believe that one day our daughter will be able to be on her own. I think about a dozen years from now, being in the empty nest with my husband. We have a lot in common. There are many things that we don't have time to share right now. Maybe we'd get back to basics in a dozen years, without the constant pressure. So there's my other fantasy, of falling in love with my husband. Of the two fantasies, the one about my husband looms larger, though it's scarier in some ways. It means taking ownership of what wasn't and what is. Ed and I are the best of friends. Right now I don't see the moons and the stars when I'm with him, but maybe someday I could.

MRS. Z

❦

Mrs. Z is a beautiful, articulate, warm thirty-seven-year-old who lives in a suburb of Cleveland with her husband of twelve years and their four children—three boys and a girl, ages six, four, two, and ten months. In her pre-mother life, she was an accountant. Her husband is a mechanical engineer with a booming business. She adores her husband and loves being a mother. She still feels the strong physical attraction for her husband that she felt when they met fourteen years ago, although their sex life has not been as spontaneous since the children came along. Yet she has a fantasy about another man, her obstetrician, that she can't shake no matter hard she tries. There are times she feels guilty, and other times when she is fearful, worrying about how vulnerable she might be to temptation. Mostly, she tries to understand the longing, given the satisfaction and happiness she derives from her life.

I'm sure this is not an atypical scenario: I fantasize about my obstetrician, who's been there for the births of all my children. I've been told that a lot of women fall in love with their obstetricians and their therapists—those men who have intimate relationships with us. I don't feel this is the case with me, though.

I find this whole situation so strange and baffling. I think it just started off, obviously, as a patient/doctor relationship, but now, unless I have a very vivid imagination, there's definitely an attraction between us. It's not one-sided. It's exciting, as well as a challenge, for me to resist crossing the boundary between flirtation and something that could be far more incendiary. I have dreams about him. I'm not in love with him, although when I say that, part of me wonders if I am trying to convince myself. I love my husband. Is it possible to love two men at once? Yes, of course it is. But I'm just infatuated with my doctor. It's not love.

Dr. Murphy (can you belicve I still call him that even in my fantasies?) is about ten years older than me. He's married. I don't know too much about his personal life, although I know he has children. From what I gather, he met his wife very early in life, and they've been married for over thirty years. I have a sense that he's at the point in his life where he's bored with everything—life, wife, work. The secretaries in his office chat with me, considering the many times I've been in the waiting room, and tell me that he works very long hours and sees very little of his wife. His kids are grown, in their early twenties. All in all, I get the feeling—both from him, when he makes any reference to his personal life, and the girls in the office—that he's not a happy, satisfied man.

I'm a practical, grounded woman. I'm not given to flights of fancy and the notion that every man I meet is smitten with me. So I know that the way Dr. Murphy relates to me is something I'm not imagining. I also know his behavior is specific to me, because I have lots of girlfriends who go to him, and we all speak candidly with one another, and no one else has the kind of connection with him that I have, and no one else has experienced the sense that he would transcend the doctor/patient relationship if given any incentive. And my friends are all attractive women who wouldn't necessarily spurn him if he made the offer.

If there was ever any doubt in my mind that his manner with me went beyond the professional, it was one day during my third pregnancy when I wasn't feeling great. I was at the hospital getting a blood test, and I called his office since I was feeling particularly queasy and having slight but palpable contractions. His receptionist said he wasn't in the office, that he was on hospital duty that day, but she would page him. In retrospect, I wonder why they paged him, because another friend of mine called his office that day and was put through to one of his partners. I wonder if he had left specific instructions in case I called. Within minutes, he called my cell phone, and since I was still at the hospital, he suggested we meet for coffee in the cafeteria and I could tell him what was wrong. As we had coffee, I felt strongly that our relationship—certainly at that moment—was not a doctor/patient relationship. There were remarks that were indisputably flirtatious: He flattered me about my appearance (even though I was six months pregnant), said I had a radiant smile, and commented that he enjoyed the way I looked at life, yet his remarks were still couched in professionalism.

It's clear that he doesn't want me to feel uncomfortable around him, and I don't. I don't feel threatened by him. He's not one of those characters out of a book like *Compromising Positions,* or one of those doctors you read about in the tabloids who have their way with patients while they're under the influence of anesthesia. He's a nice person. In some ways, I feel sorry for him, and I think that's part of my attraction. I feel that he's a little needy. I didn't tell my husband that we met for coffee that day, although I did tell him that Dr. Murphy was at the hospital and I ran into him and asked about the symptoms I had and was reassured.

I know for certain that my husband feels threatened by Dr. Murphy. When I was in labor with our fourth child, Dr. Murphy was very touchy and sweet—massaging my shoulders and my temples to relax me—and my husband was right there. At one point I needed oxygen because my heart rate had dropped, and Dr. Murphy was caressing my forehead and soothing me. My husband told me that the doctor's attitude and actions made him uncomfortable. He questioned why Dr. Murphy was so friendly and personal. To tell you the truth, I was upset with my husband during that labor and delivery, especially when my heart rate was dropping, and I felt that he should have jumped right in there and been the one to soothe and comfort me. Dr. Murphy clearly recognized the fear in my eyes as my heart rate slowed, and that was why he comforted me. It was emotional more than medical caring. I felt that my husband should have recognized my fear and known me well enough to know that I was indeed frightened. He didn't step up to the plate. I've made excuses for him—I've told myself that maybe he, too, was scared and that the care I needed at that point was out of his realm, but still.

A few months after that episode, my husband brought up the issue of Dr. Murphy again when I received a beautiful bouquet of flowers. I was so busy with the kids that I hadn't even taken off the cellophane by the time my husband came home. I just assumed the bouquet was from my husband. I was elated and immediately thanked him as he walked in the door.

"They're not from me," he said. "They must be from your doctor friend."

As it turned out, they were from my girlfriend, one of those "just because" bouquets because she knew I'd been having a bad week with the kids and that my spirits were in the doldrums. Once my husband made the remark about Dr. Murphy, I knew I needed to be careful with how I spoke about the doctor. Even when I go for a regular checkup, I think my husband gets jealous. Additionally, he has this notion that I've always wanted to *marry* a doctor. Somehow he feels that what he does for a living is a lesser profession than what doctors and lawyers do. That's my husband's insecurity.

I'm smart enough to know that if I didn't respond to Dr. Murphy's overtures, the flirtation would be aborted. There's definitely a call-and-response, and I think about that, and it makes me feel guilty. I have no illusions about the fact that in some way, I provoke his flirtation. I don't know why I enjoy responding to him, and perhaps eliciting and soliciting the exchanges between us as well.

The thing is, I'm not an unhappy housewife. I love my life. I feel very fortunate. I love my children. And I do love my husband, but there's no question that sometimes I'm a little lonely. My husband often works an eighty-hour week. He wasn't always that way. When we were first engaged and married, his business wasn't what it is now. His success is kind of a double-edged sword. Business is booming and he's successful, but I don't get to see him the way I used to when he was less prosperous. It's hard on me. I don't get a break from the kids, either. I don't really have time to do anything for myself. And my husband and I don't get to do much together.

I don't feel adored by my husband the way I used to before we had children. It wasn't so much that he gave me gifts, although he did that as well; it was more the way he talked to me, and talked about me in front of other people. I don't feel that from him anymore. I'm not blaming him. Maybe that's just the way life is. I still feel that way about him, though. I still talk in those loving ways about him. I have such respect for what he does and how hard he works for his family. I get excited about his birthday and Father's Day and Christmas. I want to give him the perfect gift and the perfect day. I would go to the ends of the earth for him, and I feel that he doesn't and wouldn't do that for me. He's just not as thoughtful as he used to be. I want little things. I'm not materialistic. He used to write me love notes and send me flowers for no reason. Sometimes, in the old days, he would just buy me a rose, and I have kept a petal of every flower and every note he ever wrote to me. He was so sweet. In some ways, I miss him so much. I miss the way we were.

I don't think he's written me a note in six years, not since our first child was born. I've told him how I feel, and he blames everything on work. He defends himself and says that he's so consumed by work that he doesn't have the time anymore. I know he's not lying. I know that he has a stressful job and long hours. He's not the kind of man who, when he's not working, goes running around with his guy friends and gambles or golfs or drinks. If anything, once a week, I urge him to get out and hang out with his friends and play a little golf because I want him to be happy.

Every so often this wonderful girl babysits for me, and my husband and I get to go out on a Saturday night, and it's so great. It brings it all back for me. I realize how much in love I am. But then we get home, and it's not the same. The kids are there, and suddenly, it's Life Interrupted. Sometimes the kids are all sleeping, but more often than not, at least one of them isn't, or they begin waking up because they have this sixth sense that I'm back. The babysitter leaves, and I'm Cinderella and everything is turning back into pumpkins. Maybe these complaints I have about my husband are my way of justifying the fact that I enjoy the flirtation with Dr. Murphy. Perhaps I have no business complaining at all.

I often ask myself why I enjoy the flirtation so much. It makes me nervous. Since I've been married, I relate to men quite differently. I can no longer put myself out there as a woman, a sexual creature: I'm a wife and a mother. Those are my definitions. Maybe the doctor is a safe outlet. But it's so crazy. There are times I actually miss him. There are times I can't wait for my next appointment. It's even occurred to me—and this is nearly sick—that if I would just get pregnant again, I could see Dr. Murphy every few weeks.

As for him having this particular specialty, it sure would make life simpler if he were a podiatrist! The truth is, he's very sexy. He's charismatic. He doesn't wear a white coat during the exams. He's there with his shirtsleeves rolled up to his elbows. It's embarrassing for me because sometimes I get excited when he examines me, and I think he must know that I am. He must love that, right? I sure would be a lot less transparent if he were just removing my corns and callouses.

Dr. Murphy is the only fantasy I've had since I've been married. I often wonder what prevents me from acting upon it. For one thing, I think he feels I'm safe because I'm too happy in my marriage to ever take the flirtation a step further. One time I brought some photographs with me from a family vacation, and I swear there was a melancholy on Dr. Murphy's face as he looked through the photos and remarked on how happy I looked. Yet if I ever gave him the opportunity, I'm not sure he would be prepared to cross the line, either. I want him to think I would never cross the line, that I am too happy to cross the line, because I don't know what I would do if he took the flirtation to the next level. I don't know that I would be able to resist the temptation. Mostly, I'm scared by the thought of crossing the line. If I knew that I could be with him without repercussion, without anyone ever knowing, without any guilt, would I do it? Probably. Mostly because I'm curious. But I would be terrified of falling in love with him. I care about him. I would want to make him happy. Maybe I'm just too much of a nurturer.

I've asked my husband if he has fantasies. I think he wants me to believe that he's more on the boring side, but he's not. He's a wonderful lover. And he's also very sexy and exciting. The problem is that he's not here enough.

I don't want to betray my husband. I don't think he deserves that sort of treatment. This is why I stop myself. Sometimes I feel so guilty just for my thoughts that I can't imagine what the guilt would be like if I ever slept with my fantasy for real. The obvious question is why don't I switch doctors? Well, he happens to be a very good doctor, and to be honest, I love the fantasy. It takes me to a place that my husband and I rarely go anymore, except on those occasional Saturday nights before the pumpkins come.

ACKNOWLEDGMENTS

This book could not have been written without the courage and candor of the twenty-six women who bared the deepest parts of their souls. Thank you for your trust.

Our deep appreciation to Peternelle van Arsdale, editor extraordinaire, who spent countless hours poring over every sentence, every nuance—until it was just right. Thanks to Kiera Hepford for tending to details.

Thanks to Ellen Archer for believing in this project right from the start and to our agent, Marcy Posner, who saw the possibilities immediately.

Thanks to Stephanie Rostan, who picked up so many pieces as we went along. Our gratitude to Beth Dickey, Katie Wainwright, Becky Kraemer, and Fauzia Burke for their commitment to getting the word about the book out to the widest possible audience.

—AL and SG

First of all, I would like to thank God.

I would like to acknowledge my children, Kevin and Kyle Lopez Dudley, for letting me be me, and for understanding and being so supportive to a creative mother—you'll never know how much I love you, you are the lights of my life forever; my sister Sharon Lopez Rhoden for everything, and Raisa and Bill Rhoden for loving her. Stephanie Gertler for all of her hard work and dedication and for always coming to the rescue; my godchildren Michelle, Cynthia, and Scott, and their dad, Garland Wood; Nancy Harris Crooks, officially my cousin for life—hugs to you all. Thanks to Edward R. Dudley Jr. for the gift of our children. And to all of the amazing women who told me their wonderful and amazing stories. I have never met any of my interviewees except by phone, and I thank you all for sharing. And to my assistant, Mendy Johnson, for "coordinatin'." To my friends who have supported me and listened to me through all of my trials and tribulations. And to everyone who believed in me . . .

God bless you all.

—AL

On a personal note, thanks, as always, to my children, David, Ellie, and Ben Schiffer—the loves of my life—for all their support and pride. You always keep me going. To Adrienne Lopez, my friend for fourteen years and now my co-author—thanks for your encouragement, sense of humor, and enthusiasm—we did it! Thank you to Mark Schiffer, for believing in my professional abilities.

Thanks to my father, Menard Gertler, for his eternal devotion to my mother and to me. And, of course, hugs to my girlfriends who save my life every day.

—SG